FROM THE HEART

FROM THE HEART

Sam Hoffer

IGUANA

Publisher: Meghan Behse
Editor: Cy Strom
Front cover design: Meghan Behse

ISBN 978-1-77180-538-4 (paperback)
ISBN 978-1-77180-539-1 (epub)

This is an original print edition of *From the Heart*.

This book is dedicated to my children, Elana and Evan.
I hope these stories and poems will let you know a little more about my
childhood, and about our family history. You are both very special to me
and I love you both very much. May life bring you much happiness, just
as you both deserve.

Dear Ronnie

We live in a world of boundless treasure
Natural wonders, creations of mankind
Perhaps the greatest, the human spirit –
The soul of our mind.
That spirit, like a fine cut stone
Reveals itself in countless facets
The richest of these –
Laughter, Love, Peace and Hope.
To each you bring new meaning
As you shower these virtues with beauty and truth
In your hands, Ronnie, they come alive –
And offer a glimpse of a better world.
May we enrich your life
As you enrich our own
And may you live beyond one hundred years
To teach us evermore of
        Laughter,
        and
        Love,
        and
        Peace,
        and
        Hope.

Table of Contents

Sam Hoffer z"l

*As told by his wife Ronnie, children Elana and Evan, and
nephew Lloyd Hoffer*

Kind. Caring. Compassionate. Thoughtful. Generous. Intelligent.
Insightful. Humorous. A husband. A father. A brother. A brother-in-law. An uncle. A cousin. A son. A historian. A teacher. A listener. A
mentor. An analyst. A friend. A colleague. A public servant. A comic.
A mensch. All of these things were Sam Hoffer.

Sam was born in 1945 in Chernowitz, Romania, the son of two
Holocaust survivors, Sali z"l and David z"l, and the brother of Leizer and
Joe. He and his parents made their way to Israel and then to Canada
where they joined Sam's brothers who had preceded them in Hoffer,
Saskatchewan. There, his parents and brothers struggled to assimilate
their European Jewish roots and Holocaust experience to a new strange
land, and Sam grew from a child to a teenager and to an adult with strong
roots in the past and yet a strong eye to the future. For the duration of his
life, Sam would seek Jewish meaning wherever he could, through his
volunteerism and in personal projects, in the Canadian context.

Sam was married to Ronnie for 48 years and was so proud of and
cared so much for her and for their children Elana and Evan. His

commitment to family extended to his and Ronnie's parents as long as they were alive and also to the larger extended family. Beyond their nieces and nephews in Canada, Sam was the linchpin of connection and communication between the extended Canadian and Israeli branches of the Hoffer family.

Always at the centre of Sam's attention were children and young adults, for whom he always had time to listen and to advise, and whom he always made sure to include in every endeavour he could.

Sam was a wonderful documentarian for whom reconstruction and preservation of family history was of key importance. Together with collecting information and photographic images of the past, he was an excellent photographer and videographer in his own right, creating albums of the family's Canadian and European history and video recordings to preserve history for his own family and others.

Sam's artistic side also included writing and poetry. His serious side was balanced with humour, notably including Yiddish comedy, which he wrote and recorded on CD. He felt no one should miss out on a chance to laugh.

Jewish history and tradition, and Jewish circumstances both in the Diaspora and in Israel, permeated Sam's thought and life in all of his relationships, artistry and activities. May his memory succeed in carrying the blessing of his spirit to others.

From the Heart

Sunrise

It appeared as an aura at first,
a canopy above the silhouette of distant hills.
A majestic radiance followed, slowly, irrepressibly,
its rays stirring the wakening heavens,
then melding into a blinding ball of light.
Perhaps it saw me too,
a mere speck on a timeless landscape,
a witness to the wonder of Creation.

First Flower

I saw it then –
Not at a fleeting glance
But truly saw it, in all its splendour
And filled my lungs 'til I could breathe no more.

A Tribute

The eyes that saw the evil
that tormented blameless souls,
will soon be gone.

The ears that heard commands
that chilled the blood,
will soon be gone.

The hearts that ceased to beat
with loved ones lost,
will soon be gone.

The minds that shattered
in fear and disbelief,
will soon be gone.

The certain knowledge
of the cruelty of man,
will soon be gone.

Who will believe us,
orphans of the truth,
when they are gone?

Fly With Me (Translation)

I soar freely in the skies
Launch my skiffs across the lake
Build bridges over houses
"Look here mother, what I make!"

Later, I search for remote peoples
In all corners of the earth
So that I can better grasp
The true meaning of our birth

All wonders since revealed
Each pondered for a clue
It's clear to me as heaven
None rivals friendship, true

Now resting by my fire
I hear children laugh and cry
A bird calls at my window
Fly with me, far and high

פֿלי מיט מיר

איך פֿלי מיר אין די הימלען
לאָז אָפּ שיפּלעך אויפֿן טײַך
בוי בריקן איבער שטיבער
'זע נאָר מאַמע ,וואָס איך מאַך'

שפּעטער, זוך איך פֿרעמדע פֿעלקער
אין די עקן פֿון דער וועלט
בעסער קענען צו פֿאַרשטיין
אין וואָס די וועלט באַשטייט

אויפֿגעדעקט שוין אַלע ווינדער
געפֿאָרשט און באַטראַכט
איז מיר קלאָר ווי בלויער הימל
פֿרײַנטשאַפֿט האָט די גרעסטע מאַכט

היינט זיצנדיק ביים פֿײַער
הער איך קינדער אין דעם הויף
זע אַ פֿויגל אין דעם פֿענצטער
ער רופֿט מיך פֿליען, ווײַט אַרויף

Without a Good-bye

"They've fallen from their nest,"
My son exclaimed in fear.
"They'll die there on the ground," he warned,
His eyes welling with tears.
I rested in my chair and sighed
Unsure of what to say.
"It's not so simple," I replied,
"Let the parents try their way."
I slept that night and the next day
Went out to greet the sky.
Just then, from underneath a shrub
Came a scarce plaintive cry.
Though faintly heard, it beckoned me
I peered beneath the bush.
And there I saw three baby birds
Amidst a deathly hush.
They gasped for air, their bodies heaved
Each struggled to hold on.
I reached out and lifted them
So helpless, one by one.
I fed them worms and water too
They slept, they woke, they stared.
I dared not leave their side for fear
Their lives were unprepared.

I built a nest all lined with grass
And placed it in a tree.
Their mother found them soon enough
Amidst loud chirps of glee.
Cautiously, I watched them grow
They saw me too each day.
Bigger, stronger they became
And braver too, I'd say.
And then one morning I remarked,
"See how that one peeks out.
It's looking for the sun today
It's peering all about."
That very day, a hot one too
I came again to see.
But they were gone and left behind
An empty nest for me.

A Portrait in Time

A Note to the Reader:
These are the imagined though not unlikely events that led
to the making of this portrait.

Seated are Vikke and Yoshia with their two children, Henia and Zelig.
Standing is Vikke's sister (name unknown).
Photograph, circa 1922.

A knock at the door. Vikke, not expecting anyone, immediately cast her eyes about to assure herself that Zelig and Henia were there and safe. She shooed them out of the room, wiping her hands on her apron to remove what remained of the dough she'd been kneading at the kitchen table.

Who could it be on a Monday morning? she wondered. Her husband Yoshia had left hours ago to the market in Viznitz with a wagonload of hay. Chava, her younger sister, was in the village delivering some mending she had done.

She went to the window, carefully moving aside an edge of the cloth curtain. It was a young man, wearing a tired black suit and hat and a closely trimmed full beard. He seemed pleasant but one could never tell. She opened the door just enough to avoid offending the stranger but without appearing to welcome him into her home.

"Hello," she said, waiting for him to explain what he wanted.

"Good afternoon and excuse me," he said, touching but not removing his hat. "My name is Yakov Katz. I'm a photographer. I'm visiting Chornohuzy to make family portraits, if you are interested."

Vikke noted the modest horse and buggy behind him. She had of course seen photographs but she had never seen a camera, much less met a photographer. She hadn't dreamt of ever having her picture taken and felt a rush of excitement as she saw a fleeting image of herself and her family posing for a portrait. She wondered what Yoshia would say.

Sensing that it was not dangerous, Zelig, four, and his sister, three, crept stealthily behind their mother, each gripping one side of her skirt while catching a glimpse of the stranger.

"Could you come back tomorrow, in the morning?" Vikke asked. "We're busy right now," she added, hoping he would not suspect that she was alone with her children.

"Of course," he replied. "I'll come at ten o'clock if that suits you."

Vikke nodded and moved to close the door. Zelig and Henia squeezed into the narrowing gap, straining to watch the man leave.

A torrent of questions followed. "Who was that, Mameh? What does he want? What is a photographer?"

Vikke tried to explain but grew impatient as her mind wandered to her husband and Chava, anticipating what they would say. Yoshia was not one for the latest gimmicks. Times were trying enough without squandering hard-earned money on frivolous things like photographs. As she thought about it, she half regretted asking the photographer to come back, not wanting to upset Yoshia if he had had a difficult day at the market. She resolved to bide her time and see how things had gone before she told him about the photographer's visit.

Not an hour later, Chava returned. She had hardly had a chance to close the door behind her when she was besieged by Henia and Zelig.

"Tanteh Chava! Tanteh Chava! We're going to have our picture taken!" exclaimed the chorus of voices. Chava bent down to embrace them, kissing their beaming faces. She glanced up at Vikke inquiringly, unable to read her expression.

"Sit down," Vikke beckoned, "I have to talk to you before Yoshia gets back. An interesting thing happened while you were away." She told Chava how she had answered the door and she described the young man who greeted her, noting that he was decently dressed and mannerly, and that he'd introduced himself as a photographer offering to make a family portrait. "I didn't want to discuss it without Yoshia here so I told him to come back in the morning. What do you think, Chava?" she asked.

Chava could tell that Vikke was excited about the idea but guessed that she was uncertain about Yoshia's reaction. "I think it would be wonderful to have a family portrait," she replied, more cautiously than she would have wanted to, reluctant to put any pressure on her sister and Yoshia.

"But will Yoshia be here in the morning?" Chava asked.

"Yes, I'm sure he'll be here. I just don't know what he'll say."

Chava got up from her chair, reflecting on the sudden appearance of this stranger. Visitors to the village were few and far between. The most common were rabbinical students who came from Viznitz to collect donations for the yeshiva. Their stay in the village, however brief, never failed to stir the imagination of the single girls. Occasionally, peddlers who also travelled the rural roads took a room at the local inn, but they were suspect, not the kind Yoshia or any family head would entrust with one of his own.

Her mind drifted to the images of the man Vikke had described. She had said that he was young and presentable. The fact that he wore a neatly trimmed beard could mean that he was religious and maybe also enlightened, modern. But he might be married. Everything, she concluded, would depend on Yoshia.

Yoshia ate contently, seated on his wagon behind his market stall. He was grateful for the cheese that Leib Drassinover, his son David's father-in-law, had brought him when he came into town. Leib had three cows and some sheep that he kept in a clearing in the forest. He made a good living selling his cheeses as well as milk, cream and butter to the townsfolk in Chornohuzy and even Viznitz.

He considered how fortunate David had been to find such a fine girl as Chaya Sura, Leib's eldest daughter. She was much younger than David and full of life, always singing and cheerful but also devoted to her parents. She would be good for David, who was hard working, a caring son but a bit too serious. Maybe Chaya Sura would teach him how to enjoy life more.

He inhaled the aroma of the thick slices of freshly baked bread and quartered the apple Vikke had sent along. It had been a good day. He had sold all of his hay to the wagoners who needed it for their horses. Nikolai had even offered him a drink of vodka to toast their deal. He was one of the regulars who relied on Yoshia for good feed at a decent price. Yoshia tried hard to keep him and the others happy. He didn't relish the thought of having to compete for new customers. He had stiff competition and being Jewish didn't help. Still, he got along well with them. It was good that he had a thick skin. He could laugh along at their jokes without forgetting why he was there.

As the afternoon began to fade, he lingered a moment in the warm sun before preparing to leave. He was not in a rush. He would be home well before dark.

He fed and watered his horse and checked again that the money was secure in its place under the seat. Pulling away from the market stall, he nodded to the others who were loading what remained of their wares.

There had been no rain for two weeks so the road was dry and easier on his horse and wagon. As he drew closer to the countryside, he began to hum the songs of the Shabbos prayers that he found so comforting. His mind wandered to days long ago when he was a small boy and had gone to the synagogue with his father on Shabbos mornings. Most of all, he had enjoyed sitting beside him, wrapping a hand in his father's tallis and inhaling the musty smell of the old books from which the men studied. With these thoughts flooding his mind, Yoshia's voice rose to the heavens.

From afar, he noticed the tall stalks stir just before three men emerged from the corn field along the road. He couldn't tell at this distance who they were. They were being boisterous, laughing and slapping each other good naturedly on the back. It would be only minutes before they saw him approaching.

He came closer, maintaining a steady pace, his horse plodding along, oblivious to the men just steps away. Yoshia recognized one of them. Vasily lived half a kilometre from his home. He was the youngest son of the Ukrainian neighbour he'd known since both of them were boys. They had played together until they became teenagers and then they had drifted apart. But to this day, Sasha had been friendly to him and Vikke, always greeting them respectfully and asking about their children.

Yoshia hoped that a wave and a smile would be enough for Vasily and his friends to let him pass.

Vasily put up his hand and kept it there, signalling Yoshia to stop.

"Good afternoon," he greeted Yoshia. "It's good to see you on such a fine day."

"Good afternoon, Vasily," Yoshia replied, smiling. "It's good to see you too. How is your father?"

"Fine," Vasily replied, as he held the horse's bridle, his friends walking casually around to the back of the wagon.

"How was your day at the market?" Vasily asked, glancing at his friends. "With such fine weather you must have brought a good load and gotten an excellent price for your hay."

"It's been a good day, thank you, Vasily. I'm looking forward to getting home and putting my feet up with my family."

"What's the rush?" chimed in one of Vasily's friends. "No time for a chat?" Yoshia, feeling uneasy, looked for some reassurance from Vasily, but he avoided Yoshia's gaze.

"Of course," Yoshia replied, "in fact how about a drink before I move on?" He got up from the seat and flipped open the lid to take out the bottle of vodka he kept there for the occasional shot. Vasily peered into the open box, his eyes fixing on the small leather pouch that he was sure held Yoshia's money. But he said nothing as Yoshia pretended not to notice Vasily's searching eyes and closed the lid.

He handed them the bottle, grinning approvingly as each of them took a generous swig. A small price to pay, he thought, though he worried that the drink might go to their heads. Vasily drank last, wiping his mouth with the back of his hand, and returned the bottle to Yoshia.

"You'd better get going, old man," he said, giving the horse a friendly slap on the rear. "It's getting late and you never know who you might run into on the road," he laughed loudly, the others joining in. Yoshia lost no time in flicking the reins, urging his horse on. He casually saluted the young men who stood aside to let him pass. Vasily, still laughing, shouted, "And give my best to beautiful Chava!"

Yoshia stepped up the pace. He'd had enough, not wanting to chance an encounter with another gang of anti-Semites. He wasn't so concerned for himself but he knew that none of them was safe, Vikke, his kids and certainly not Chava who had obviously caught Vasily's eye. And they weren't alone. Only a year ago, a herd of men in town had ganged up on a Jewish farmer and his wife, and in a drunken stupor burned their home to the ground, nearly killing them inside.

Worst of all was the constant taunting. He'd had a steady diet of it from when he was a child, going to cheder. And now he feared for Zelig and Henia. It would be impossible to protect them day and night.

As the sun set behind the surrounding forest, he pulled into his yard. Vikke came out to greet him, offering him a drink of ice cold water and a taste of the potato pudding she'd just baked.

"Hello Vikkele," he said smiling gratefully as he savoured his favourite treat. "How are the children?"

"They are well," she answered, her eyes searching for a hint of how his trip had gone. He appeared to be tense, but she chose not to probe. She'd let him tell her if there was anything wrong.

"The market was good," Yoshia said, as he removed the harness from his horse. "I sold all the hay, most of it to Nikolai and at a good price."

Vikke smiled, wondering all the more about the strain in Yoshia's voice. "I'm going inside," she said. "Come in soon. It's getting dark."

Yoshia finished his chores, then led the horse into the barn, and locked him up for the night.

Inside, Vikke, Chava and the children were already seated, waiting. After washing his hands, Yoshia sat down in his chair at the head of the table and recited the blessing over the bread to begin their meal.

"Well, children, what do you have to tell me?" Yoshia asked in a jovial voice, hoping to disguise his lingering unease. He caught Zelig's eye just as the boy glanced quizzically at his mother.

Anticipating Yoshia's question, Vikke said, "We had a surprise visitor today. A photographer."

Yoshia looked up, waiting for her to go on.

"He came to the door mid-morning. He said his name is Yakov Katz and offered to make a family portrait for us. I didn't know whether you would want to or if we could afford it, so I told him only that he should come back tomorrow, thinking that he could discuss it with you."

"Are you sure," Yoshia asked, "that he wasn't some fraudster looking for trouble?"

"He seemed pleasant enough," Vikke replied. "He was dressed respectably, he had a full beard, neatly trimmed, and he was very polite." Hearing no immediate objection from Yoshia she added, "He said he would come at ten."

The idea of making a portrait was as far removed from Yoshia's mind as climbing the Tower of Babel. But he could tell that there had been a lot of excitement in his absence. He wondered whether Chava had also met this photographer. He didn't want to ask for fear of appearing to doubt Vikke. Chava had said nothing so far but he suspected that beneath that silence she, most of all, was hoping he would approve of tomorrow's visit.

"All right," he smacked the table with the palm of his hand. "If we're going to have a guest, then let's have a guest! We will invite him for some refreshments, perhaps even to our midday meal and let him tell us what's going on in the world. But," he cautioned, looking at Vikke, his face turning serious, "I'm not promising anything about a portrait."

"I love you, Tateh!" Henia shouted as both children cheered, their heads nearly colliding in a frenzy of scheming. The twinkle in Vikke's eye, which he knew so well, revealed her excitement. Chava eagerly fetched the cookies from the stove, baked to welcome Yoshia home, and set them on the table, returning just as quickly to boil some water for tea.

Yoshia observed his family's joy and suppressed the bitterness of the afternoon. He had a great deal to be thankful for. He'd had a good day at the market and he was here, surrounded by his family in his own home. There was little more that a man could ask for.

Yakov was up in time to join the men in morning services at the small one-room wooden structure that served as the village synagogue. It wasn't much of a building, more of a shack with a single window, a roof that threatened to leak at any time, and walls that sagged from years of service and a patchwork of repairs. Chaim, the shammes, who had been so generous to put him up in his one-room flat overnight, clearly did what he could to hold the building together using his ingenuity and the few coins that the regulars found to spare on days when they had yahrzeit or, with God's help, a stroke of good fortune.

As they neared the synagogue, Yakov noted the brilliant sun rising above the tops of the distant hills, its warming rays mingling with the cool morning breeze. He took a deep breath, filling his chest with hope.

He smiled gratefully at Chaim as they came to the doorway. "Thank you again for letting me stay at your place last night. I had a very restful sleep." He was being honest, despite having spent the night on the floor on top of a makeshift bed of blankets and rags.

Chaim nodded in acknowledgement, immediately searching to see if any of the men had arrived. Reb Moyshe, the eldest of the regulars, was already there, dressed in his tallis and tefillin, hunched over one of the holy books, studying fervently under the still-dim light at the window. Chaim walked over to him with Yakov, knowing that while Moyshe would not ordinarily want to be disturbed in his studies, nothing was more important than welcoming a stranger into their midst.

Chaim stood respectfully at Reb Moyshe's side, waiting for him to look up before speaking. After a moment or two, Reb Moyshe caught sight of Chaim out of the corner of his eye and turned to face the two men.

"A good morning to you, Reb Moyshe," Chaim said, in a loud voice, betraying Reb Moyshe's failing hearing. "We have a guest this morning. His name is Yakov Katz!" Reb Moyshe looked from one man to the other and slowly broke into a welcoming smile. "Sholem aleykhem," he said, "where do you come from, young man?"

"I am from Chernowitz," Yakov replied. "I came here only yesterday and am passing through Chornohuzy on my way to other villages."

"And what brings you here?"

"I am a photographer, Reb Moyshe," he said, speaking slowly.

Reb Moyshe looked at Chaim. He nodded knowingly but said nothing, not sure if he'd heard the strange word correctly and not wanting to offend their guest. "May you have good fortune in your endeavours," he offered, and returned to his studies.

As men filed in, Chaim introduced Yakov to them, one by one. They welcomed him warmly, gathering around, eager to hear the purpose of his visit and to glean some news from the outside world.

After services were over, as the men conversed while putting away their taleysim and tefillin, Reb Hersh the butcher and Reb Zalman the tailor, both clearly better off than most of the others, invited him to their homes to meet their families and explore possibilities for a portrait. Yakov was encouraged by their interest. It had been a long journey. He needed some fruit for his labours.

In honour of Yakov, Chaim took out the bottle of schnapps that he'd kept hidden in his jacket and unwrapped the portion of honey cake that the baker's wife had given him the previous evening.

When all had filled their glasses, Chaim raised his and pronounced, "May your journey, Yakov, be fruitful and your stay in out modest village bring you success. To good health and peace, l'chaim!" The men responded with a resounding, "L'chaim!" and downed their liquor, each smacking his lips, officially marking the conclusion of the morning service.

Yakov returned to Chaim's flat, retrieved his horse and buggy, loaded his equipment and set out for Yoshia's home.

Yakov felt that he had plenty of time to get to his destination. A brief detour into the countryside on a blissful day would sharpen his creative instincts for the work ahead. The truth was that nature photography was his passion and that the verdant slopes of the Carpathian Mountains never failed to quicken his heart.

The road from Chaim's flat took him to a main street, which, in fact, was a dirt road only a bit more travelled than the track in front of the synagogue. The street took him within minutes to the edge of the village. He maintained a leisurely pace, taking in the small orchards of plums, pears, cherries and apples, fruits that grew in abundance on these fertile lands. A warm gust of wind enveloped him in the aroma of the ripening crops and made his mouth water. How he longed for these sights, the occasional wildlife, the songs of countless birds in the trees. Chernowitz was rich in commerce and culture, he conceded, but his heart was deeply rooted in the countryside.

He thought of how much he would have wanted to enjoy this moment with Rivka. They had grown close in the past year, sharing hopes for the future. She, developing her love of the violin, while he explored his passion for photography. They had met at a gathering to celebrate their mutual friend Esther's engagement and, after proper introductions, had arranged to meet, first in Esther's company and then alone. They knew that their families would not approve but they took their chances, hoping to be safe from prying eyes.

He wished that Rivka would overcome her reservations about living in the country. He understood her need to be among people, especially colleagues who shared her passion for music. He had witnessed her rapture during a solo performance and her genuine delight when she applauded a friend. She understood his passion, too. His burning desire to capture the beauty of nature. Yet she feared that life away from the city would spell the end of what to her was more than a career. It was her life.

He climbed down from his buggy and, having removed his camera from its case, walked toward the cherry trees that bordered the side of the road. He strolled into the orchard, looking back occasionally to check on his horse. He regarded the trees with awe, their age, their gnarled limbs, the ruby-red colour of the cherries soon ready to be picked. A particular tree caught his eye. As always, it was that indescribable combination of light, shape, colour, texture and context that made it magical. He stood under the tree and noted the striking contrast of the wizened branches against the expanse of vibrant blue. He caught sight of a solitary white cloud drifting directly over the tree, breaking up the singular colour of the sky. Its presence threw the branches into a mixture of relief. It struck Yakov that this imperfection was the perfect image. He took picture after picture quickly, with movements that were second nature to him now, assuring himself that there wasn't an angle or a perspective that he might have missed. He could perform magic later in the dark room but nothing would replace what his eyes now saw.

Getting back into the buggy, Yakov was pleased with his prize. It would make a fitting gift for Rivka, a token to compensate for his absence.

As Chava tossed and turned trying to fall asleep, her thoughts drifted repeatedly to her friend Tushka. They had known each other since they were small children in school and had continued their friendship through the years, not quite best friends but always taking an interest in each other. They had grown closer when Tushka's older sister Chaya Sura married David, Yoshia's eldest son.

Chava admired Tushka's resolve in moving away from Chornohuzy to make a life for herself in Chernowitz. It had a large Jewish community, yeshivas and a host of Jewish enterprises, large and small. Tushka's father had encouraged her and had placed his trust in his brother, a successful businessman in the city, to give her a home and make her welcome.

It had come as a surprise to Chava when she received a letter almost a month earlier from Tushka, inviting her to come and visit. She would stay with her at her uncle's place where there was plenty of room and generous hospitality. Together, Tushka suggested, they would explore the city, Tushka offering to introduce her to the cultural attractions and historical sights. They might even enjoy a meal at Tushka's favourite restaurant in the Jewish district. And her aunt, who had lived in Chernowitz all her life, might arrange for them to meet some of the wealthy ladies with whom she met regularly. "Who knows where that might lead?" Tushka teased. The possibility of a suitor was, of course, an ever-present hope. But it was the last few lines of the letter that had made Chava's heart race:

Chava, I know that you have always liked to make ladies' clothes. You are very creative and a good designer. You'll never have a chance to use your talents in Chornohuzy. But here, where fashion is on every woman's lips, you can have a future. Let me at least introduce you to the owner of the company I work for and see what happens. At worst we'll have a wonderful visit together.

Chava had hardly been able to contain her excitement. She was already eighteen and beginning to feel that her uneventful life was leading nowhere. She saw no possibility of breaking out of Chornohuzy, dependent as she was on her sister Vikke and her generous husband Yoshia, for a home. Her parents had passed away, leaving her little by way of independent means, and without the support of someone to sponsor her, it would be impossible for her to make a life of her own in another place.

She recalled her conversation with Vikke, to whom she had read the letter only after she'd studied every word in it a dozen times in the privacy of her room. Vikke had been conspicuously silent for some minutes afterward. She had obviously weighed her reaction, having had mixed feelings about the prospect of Chava leaving.

In the end, she had approached Chava, and putting her arms around her and kissing her on the cheek, had said, "You deserve to be happy. That's all I want for you. So you have to be careful and you have to be sure." Her sister's eyes had visibly teared up as she let Chava go and turned away.

"I don't want to leave you, Vikke," Chava had said. "The idea of being with strangers in a big city so far from home terrifies me."

"You'll get used to it. You need a new life. Tushka is right, you have amazing talents that you should put to work. Not here, but where you can flourish. And where, with God's help, you will find your match. We'll miss you greatly, Chava, especially me. But maybe you'll be our reason to get away and come to visit the big city!"

Chava had been certain that Vikke was only being kind.

They had discussed the letter at length, imagining all the exciting possibilities, Vikke secretly rejoicing in the happiness that these dreams brought to her sister's heart. After a time, they had agreed that nothing more would be done until they told Yoshia about the letter.

Chava recalled Yoshia's distressing reaction. He had said nothing at first. Finally, he had told them that he would think about it and would discuss it further in a day or two. The days and hours were an eternity as he remained tight-lipped, refusing to tell even Vikke anything of his thoughts. It was not until two days later, after the children had gone to bed, that they all sat down to talk at the table

Yoshia had begun by recounting Chava's early years with them, when she was much younger and he and Vikke were newly married. The sudden passing of Chava's mother had left her alone and frightened. Yoshia reminded them of how painful the adjustment had been for Chava, despite the fact that Vikke was her sister, and of how difficult it had been for Vikke to gain Chava's trust. "Now," he had said, "you are a grown woman, Chava. You have a right to your own future."

Then, still looking at Chava, he had continued, "I paid Leib Drassinover a visit. I did it without telling you because I didn't want you to worry. I wanted to know from him, face to face, about Tushka's circumstances, about his brother Itzik and his wife and whether he thought it was safe for you to go. Chernowitz is a big city, Chava," he had cautioned. "There are many unscrupulous characters, and while I have total confidence in you, I couldn't live with myself if something went wrong."

"After I asked him all my questions and we'd enjoyed a wonderful spread of bread and cheese and a shnaps, Leib revealed to me that he already knew that you might be getting an invitation from Tushka. In fact, he said, his brother had written to him some time earlier, asking if he could confirm what Tushka had told him of your talent as a dressmaker. Leib said that he had discussed it with his wife, who knew your work, and then had given you a glowing recommendation. He was not at all surprised to hear of the invitation.

"As for my concerns, Leib told me not to worry. He said that Itzik, whom I never knew well even when he lived in Chornohuzy, is an honourable man, successful in his business, and would treat you like the daughter he saw in Tushka."

Chava had paid no heed to the growing ache in her hand from Vikke's tightening grip as they absorbed Yoshia's words. She had been close to tears with joy when he locked eyes with Vikke, and with a generous smile ordered, "Let's have a drink, a l'chaim. Our Chava's life is about to begin. May it be blessed."

When Chava awoke, the sun was already shining brightly. Vague memories of her thoughts during the night lingered as she suddenly remembered that the photographer would be coming at ten. It was late and she had to help Vikke prepare, especially as they were hoping that he would stay for the midday meal. She stepped into the kitchen, finding Vikke already bent over the table, cutting up vegetables.

"I'm sorry I slept in, Vikke. All night I tossed and turned and then I must have fallen asleep just before morning."

"It's fine. I have most things ready. The bread is baking and the soup is on the stove. If you want to prepare some fruit, that would be good."

Chava made herself a slice of bread, butter and prune jam, then chose some fruit from the basket to set on the table.

6

The sun was already well above the horizon when Yakov rounded the bend in the road and saw Yoshia's home on a small hill in the clearing below. He had come upon it unexpectedly when he had approached Chornohuzy the previous day, and on an impulse had driven up to the door and knocked.

The lady had greeted him coolly, he'd thought, but the arrival of a stranger with a horse and buggy had clearly been unexpected. Being cautious was wise, especially if, as he suspected, she'd been alone with the children he had seen hiding behind her, watching him with a mixture of apprehension and wonder.

As he approached the yard, he saw a man carrying a bucket toward the barn. The man looked up and, seeing the horse and buggy approach, slowly set the bucket on the ground and waited. The children lost no time running to their father's side.

Yakov drew his horse to a halt, simultaneously touching the brim of his hat and saying, "Sholem aleykhem."

"Aleykhem sholem," Yoshia responded warmly, introducing himself. "You must be Yakov."

"Yes," he replied, climbing down from his buggy to shake Yoshia's outstretched hand. "I was here yesterday. I believe I spoke to your wife. She was kind enough to ask me to come back today. I hope you don't mind." He reached back to the buggy and retrieved a leather pouch that he slung over his shoulder.

"I understand you are a photographer," Yoshia nodded, encouraging Yakov to go on.

"Yes, from Chernowitz. I'm visiting some of the villages, making family portraits," and after a slight pause, he added, "this morning I had the pleasure of praying at the synagogue and meeting some of the men. Chaim, the shammes, was particularly welcoming."

"Oh, good," Yoshia answered smiling broadly. "I go there on Shabbos. During the week, I pray at home."

Seeing Yoshia glance down at his bucket of water, Yakov said, "I apologize, Reb Yoshia, I interrupted your work."

"Not at all. Why don't we tie up your horse here, near the barn, give him some food and water and then go to the house?" Then turning to the children, he said, "Zelig, go and tell your mother that our guest is here." Zelig and Henia sped off to the house, racing to be the first to break the news. Yakov followed Yoshia's direction while Yoshia took the bucket into the barn to water his horse.

Yoshia prided himself on being a good judge of character. He was sure that there was more to this young man's story, but he had a good feeling about him. As they strolled toward the house, Yoshia said, "I've asked my wife to prepare a place for you at our midday meal. We would be pleased if you would stay and join us."

"That's very kind of you. I don't want to intrude or be a burden," Yakov replied.

"On the contrary, Yakov, it will give us a chance to hear about what's going on in the world. We rarely have the pleasure of a guest from the big city."

Yoshia opened the door and ushered Yakov in, at the same time announcing their arrival. He was sure that the women had been anxiously anticipating this moment, and that they would be more than ready to receive their guest.

Vikke greeted Yakov with a warm smile. So much more welcoming, Yakov observed, than the previous day. Seeing Chava walking toward them, Yoshia encouraged her to come forward, saying, "And this is Chava, my wife's sister."

"I'm very pleased to meet you," Yakov said.

"Yakov," Yoshia announced, "has accepted my invitation to stay and eat with us."

"We're very glad to have you," Vikke said. "I hope you'll enjoy our cooking." Smiling at Yakov, Chava nodded in agreement. Yakov had no doubt from the aromas filling the room that the meal would be both succulent and generous.

"Please, Yakov," Yoshia said, "take a chair at the table, and let's talk."

Vikke gathered up the children and led them outside, explaining in a hushed voice that for the next little while they would have to play outdoors, while the adults talked in the house. If they were very quiet and well behaved, she whispered, there would be a special treat for them later.

Yakov enjoyed Yoshia's down-to-earth and friendly manner. It set him at ease in the plain but warm surroundings of this small home. They took their seats at a square table near the wood-burning stove on which he saw several pots warming. A doorway led from the kitchen to another area, probably the sleeping quarters. Bright morning sunlight lit up the room and streamed onto the worn but impeccably clean wooden floor.

"I see that you're carrying a pouch, Yakov," Yoshia said. "Do you possibly have some portraits of families you could show us? I'm very interested in seeing what you do."

Yakov welcomed the question. It saved him the awkwardness of bringing up the subject and gave him an opportunity to show off his work. He carefully undid the straps of the pouch that Rivka had given him as a gift when he embarked on his trip and removed the album of photographs of the past year. He set the album on the table and opened it to the first portrait.

Yoshia studied the pictures. They were admirable photographs, capturing not only the appearance of the people in vivid detail, but also possessing a depth that offered a glimpse into their character. The hint of a smile here, exaggerated posture there, a cane in the hand at a determined angle, children grinning at a machine they had never seen before.

Yoshia's mind wandered as he slowly turned the pages. Beautiful as the portraits were, they somehow made him uneasy. He struggled to understand his feelings but said nothing, nodding approvingly. It occurred to him that it was the silence of the photographs that troubled him, the stillness, the tranquility and comfort they portrayed. His throat tightened as an image of Vasily flashed before his eyes. Their encounter on the road played across the pages. The brazen disregard Vasily and his friends had displayed for Yoshia, for his person, for his right to be there, undisturbed. The not-so-subtle threats. The hint of trouble facing Chava. His fear for his children. He sensed an impending danger, a misplaced trust, as he looked into the eyes of the people who stared back at him from the pages. He could not accept the safety, the security, and permanence that the pictures promised.

"Have you run into any trouble on the roads, Yakov?" Yoshia asked, without looking up.

Yakov was somewhat startled by the question. He had been following Yoshia's gaze as he reviewed the pictures, but had no idea as to why Yoshia was asking this or what in the photographs had prompted the question. In truth, he'd had run-ins with some small gangs of wandering youths but had managed to extricate himself without harm. He was reluctant to discuss these experiences and answered simply, "It's been fairly peaceful. I don't travel late in the day and I stay on well-travelled roads." He hoped that that would suffice.

Yoshia nodded, certain that Yakov was not telling him everything. "Do you think we're in danger, Yakov?" he continued, looking into Yakov's eyes. "I have a fear that we're living in a lull before a storm. Maybe I'm wrong, but as I look at your beautiful photographs, I fear that all this may be temporary, an illusion. That at a whim, the world will turn against us like so many times before."

Vikke suspected that Yoshia's jarring words were not random thoughts, and that something must have transpired, perhaps at the market the day before, to prompt these questions. She was convinced that this explained the tension she had seen on Yoshia's return. She would ask him, but clearly now was not the time.

Yakov listened intently. Yoshia's concern was valid. Despite the generally peaceful relationship with the broader community, there was plenty of evidence of hatred in the city. Jews were ultimately accepted at the pleasure of everyone else, it seemed. Yet they survived, drawing their strength from their own community. It helped that Chernowitz had a large Jewish population. It enjoyed a vibrant religious and social life and a diverse and successful representation among the professions, trades and businesses.

"I understand your worry," Yakov answered, trying not to sound patronizing. "But in Chernowitz, things have been calm. We have a thriving Jewish community, but we also carry on our lives with the people around us and, as long as we're careful, we manage to get along." Pausing a moment to reflect, Yakov added, "They need us, Reb Yoshia. I can't imagine that the Gentile community would ever turn against us."

Yoshia knew that he could mount many arguments to refute what Yakov had said. History did not support Yakov's trust. But he saw no point in a debate. He'd gotten the gist of the young man's thinking. His portraits revealed his faith in a stable, even promising future. Yoshia was sure that his outlook reflected more the naïveté and optimism of youth than the reality of what Yoshia saw around him.

Chava absorbed every word that Yakov uttered about life in the big city. She was going there, but was not about to reveal that to him, for fear that it might be misunderstood. Undeterred by Yoshia's concerns, her excitement grew as she imagined a rich and active life in this urban centre, a window on the world!

Aware that his worries were about to overshadow the joy of the occasion, Yoshia marshalled his resolve, and pronounced, "Yakov, you're a fine young man and I like your work. As long as you keep the cost within reason, let's do a portrait. But I want it done now. You tell us what we have to do."

Vikke and Chava were ecstatic, exchanging glances, relieved at Yoshia's words. They smiled gratefully at him, listening closely as Yakov spoke.

Yakov took them back to the photographs. He drew attention to the formality of the portraits, the people appearing in their finest clothing. He suggested something similar, always leaving the option open in case they preferred something more casual, or simply did not have the fashionable clothes that others, especially his subjects in the city, wore.

"We'll get dressed up," Vikke declared. "I want us to look our best." Yoshia said nothing, continuing to contemplate the pictures, but heard clearly the determination in Vikke's voice. "Do you agree, Chava?" she asked.

"Yes, I would like a formal picture. Something we can remember, something special," she replied, glancing at Yakov who caught her eye just before she looked away.

"Alright then," Yoshia responded. "Yakov, we'll need some time to freshen up and then we'll get started."

Yakov readily agreed. He looked forward to roaming around the yard, watching the few animals, and taking in the primitive surroundings.

"I'll be outside," he said. "Just let me know when you're ready and I'll bring in my equipment."

7

"I like him," Vikke said to Yoshia, as if he had been waiting for her appraisal. "He's very artistic! I love his pictures."

"Yes, I agree, Vikke, and the next thing you'll tell me is that he's handsome, and then you'll ask me if he's attached. The answer is I don't know. I see no sign of it. But you're right, I like him too."

"Should we tell him that Chava is going to Chernowitz? What if it's meant to be, Yoshia, if we only help a little to make it happen?"

"I think we should leave it up to Chava. If she wants him to know, she'll find a way to tell him." Vikke wasn't so sure that Chava could do it on her own. She thought back to her own life in Viznitz when she and Chava were single and at home with their parents. She had been twenty-three when her father sought help from Malka the matchmaker, worried that she would remain unmarried, with no future. She had been wary of the process, but with assurances from her father that she would not have to agree to any match she did not want, she went along with it, however skeptically.

Yoshia had been the very first prospect. Vikke's parents had heard in detail the background of this man who, they later told her, was from a nearby village called Chornohuzy. She had been aware of it, but she knew no one who lived outside of her birthplace, Viznitz. Then she was told the sad tale of Yoshia's wife having passed away and Yoshia being left alone. He did have children but they were all adults and no longer lived with him. He was a fine man, the matchmaker had said, religious and hard working. He had a small, simple home, carried on a modest business selling hay, and was well thought of in his community.

Vikke had found it all interesting but not appealing. Although she had had few opportunities, she had not stopped imagining a more promising future. Despite her reluctance, she agreed to meet the man and then give her father her answer.

When at last they had met at her parents' home, it was his charcoal eyes that had left her spellbound. His palpable intensity had been remarkably at odds with the softness of his voice and his gentle manner. She had listened as he spoke to her father about life in Chornohuzy, his work and his children, and was struck by his youthfulness, despite the full life that he'd already lived. She tried to guess his age, difficult to do with the full beard that he wore but, without staring, she concluded that he must be in his forties, twenty or so years older than her. The thought shocked her at first, but she put it in the back of her mind. The excitement that she felt troubled her more.

Their lives in Chornohuzy had at first been simple but happy. Though it had taken her some time to adjust to living in the countryside, there were the compensating pleasures of nature and the slower pace of rural life that nurtured her relationship with Yoshia. She had missed her sister terribly but Viznitz was only a few kilometres away. Occasional trips to visit her family had been just enough for them to feel that they were all still a part of one another's lives.

Everything had changed with the tragic death of her father in a logging accident while harvesting timber in the mountains. Within months, her ailing mother's health had deteriorated further. A year later, her untimely passing had left Chava alone, her life shattered. For her part, Vikke had been unable to shake the guilt of having left her parents. She had been the one they'd leaned on in times of need, especially when her mother's health had failed. She had been more than a sister to Chava, providing a source of security and comfort when her mother was unwell and her father far from home. After the loss of their parents, Vikke had done all she could to restore Chava's life by making her a part of the home that she and Yoshia had just begun to shape.

A warm feeling coursed through her as she thought of her own two children, Henia and Zelig, the apples of her eye, and loved by Yoshia as if they were his first-born. Even his grown children embraced them with all their hearts.

Vikke was lost in thought when Chava called to ask for help. A sleeve in her dress had caught and torn near the wrist. They tossed superstition aside as Vikke took out needle and thread and carefully secured the seam.

"Good as new," Vikke declared proudly. "Now let's get this beauty in front of the camera."

"Shhh, you'll embarrass me," Chava said, rebuking Vikke. "He might hear."

"I want him to hear," Vikke teased, poking Chava in the ribs. "I like him and so does Yoshia, but don't tell him I told you."

"Really, Vikke? I didn't know you two were talking about him. He is handsome. But who knows if he's already involved with someone?"

"We won't know unless we test the waters," Vikke replied, winking.

Yoshia knocked on Chava's door. Before he could speak, Vikke announced, "We're almost ready, Yoshia. You can tell Yakov that he can bring his equipment in and get set up."

Yoshia, groomed and wearing his black suit, stepped outside, and found Yakov seated in his buggy, reading.

"Come in, Yakov," Yoshia beckoned, "the ladies are almost ready, so you can begin."

Yakov looked up. This was a transformed Yoshia. Dressed in his finest, his beard combed and trimmed and his shoes polished, he retained a strong physical presence, cloaked in a mantle of aristocracy. Yakov smiled. "You look very distinguished, Reb Yoshia, if you don't mind my saying so."

"Thank you for your compliment, young man. Now before I change my mind, come in and bring your equipment."

– 8 –

"Chava, please help me with the children," Vikke said. She had dressed them, Henia in her frilly white dress and Zelig in a smart sailor's suit. But they already needed freshening up. It took only a minute for them to become dishevelled. Henia especially was a handful, wanting to follow Yakov around and see everything that he was doing.

"Is that the camera?" Henia asked, pointing to the black box on the tripod as Yakov set up the backdrop.

"Yes, that's the camera. I'll stand behind it and point it at you. Then I'll push a button and it will take your picture."

"Will it hurt us?"

"No, but there will be a big flash of light that will be very bright for your eyes."

"I'm going to shut my eyes," she whispered to Zelig, beside her. He shook his head but said nothing. He took her by the hand and led her to the bedrooms. Chava was calling them to come and get ready.

Yakov's camera was set up, his lights and backdrop in position. They had covered the window and moved the furniture around to make room for the equipment, allowing just enough space for themselves.

"Where would you like us?" Yoshia asked.

Yakov had thought about this at length. It was going to be a formal picture and they had dressed appropriately, but there was also an irrepressible informality about these people. He decided that the children would stand, though he knew that stopping them from squirming and moving out of position might be a challenge.

"I would like you, Reb Yoshia, and your wife, to sit side by side, here." They took their seats in the chairs that were already in place.

"Now, Chava, I would like you to stand beside your sister."

Yakov stepped back to take a critical look.

Again looking at Chava, he said, "Please step behind your sister just a bit and rest your hand on the top of her chair."

"You look nice, Tanteh Chava," Henia declared. "I'm going to keep your picture when you go to the city."

Yakov pretended not to hear but suspected that "the city" meant Chernowitz. He wondered what Henia was referring to, but said nothing.

Vikke found the sudden silence awkward, and said, as if in reply to Yakov's unasked question, "Chava is going to Chernowitz in a few weeks. It seems that all of us are already preparing to miss her."

Turning to Chava, Yakov said, "It's a wonderful city. I hope you have a chance to stay there long enough to enjoy it."

"I'm looking forward to it very much," Chava answered. "I'm going to visit a close friend who has promised to show me all the sights."

Not wanting to probe any further or appear to be forward, Yakov only smiled, turning to the positioning of the children. Vikke had drawn Henia close to her when she had unexpectedly announced Chava's impending departure, and Zelig stood in front of his father, Yoshia's hands enveloping his arms. They seemed comfortable and natural in front of their parents.

Yakov moved behind his camera. He was pleased with what he saw. Formal yet intimate. The absence of smiles, as he had instructed them, would give the portrait a sense of timelessness in years to come.

He asked them to remain as erect as possible. Good posture was vital to complementing the seriousness of their faces and the formality of their dress. Chava, Vikke and Yoshia straightened up, their eyes fixed on the camera. The children were another matter. Henia put her little feet together but insisted on leaning back against her mother. Zelig, his knee bent and arms cocked, stood ready to escape.

Quiet descended on the dimly lit room as Yakov rested his hand on the camera.

Yakov regarded the family, ready, poised. He saw Chava, beautiful, statuesque, leaning slightly on her outstretched arm as she held the back of Vikke's chair, perhaps her natural instinct to be close to her sister. The light-coloured dress, gathered at the waist, accentuated her shapely figure and stood in stark contrast to her black hair that was pulled tightly back. She looked confident, ready for the challenges ahead, perhaps anticipating her adventure in Chernowitz. What would she do there, he wondered, while she visited her friend? Would she consider a life in the city? She seemed capable of a great deal, not bound by the ground she stood on. The radiance in her face struck him as the energy of a mature woman embarking on life with self-assurance and grace.

Vikke sat tall as if to overcome her short stature, so evident beside the towering Yoshia. Her white blouse sparkled against the black satin collar of her dress and set her face in sharp relief. Her black hair, like Chava's, was dramatically pulled back. She exuded determination and strength, a woman steadfast in her mission to care for those around her, the emotional anchor to her family. She held restless Henia with only one hand, perhaps caring less for the perfection of the portrait than for the joy of the moment. Her casual grip on her purse conveyed a comfort with herself and the image she portrayed.

Yakov's generous beard and black hair drew attention to his high forehead and wide-set eyes. His penetrating gaze into the camera lens displayed a deep intensity. This was no casual photograph he had agreed to. This was an attempt at capturing for all time what he feared might be an ephemeral moment. Yoshia wanted more than preservation; he wanted survival. His hands, gripping Zelig's arms, revealed a man holding on to all that was dear to him, to life itself, in the face of a threatening world.

Yakov pressed the shutter.

Epilogue

In the years following the making of this portrait, the people in the photograph and others who appeared in the story became victims of the Holocaust. This is what is known of their fate.

Those in the portrait:

Yoshia, Vikke and Henia: All three, after being expelled from their home in Chornohuzy, were killed in 1941 by the Germans and their Romanian collaborators.

Chava: Her real name is not known. Nothing is known of her life.

Zelig: Survived the Shargorod ghetto in Transnistria with his wife Freda. Their first daughter, Bat Rut, was born in Shargorod. After the war, they emigrated to Israel where a second daughter, Nitzhona, was born.

Others in the story:

Yakov: His real name is not known. Nothing is known of his life.

Leib: Murdered near his home by local Ukrainians in 1941, the first casualty in the Jewish community of Chornohuzy.

Itzik: Nothing is known of his fate.

Tushka: Survived the Bershad ghetto in Transnistria with her husband Zoniu. They emigrated to Israel after the war and had a son and daughter, Zvi and Anina.

David and Chaya Sura: Survived the Shargorod ghetto in Transnistria, together with their two teenage sons, Leizer and

Jossel. The family, including a third son, Sam, born after the war, settled in the Sonnenfeld Colony, a Jewish farming community in the Province of Saskatchewan, in Canada.

The remaining people portrayed in the story are fictitious.

Selections from

An Uncertain Dawn:
My Days on the Prairies

a memoir

Before the Beginning (Ostia)

Irko, Daniel and I danced from foot to foot on the burning sidewalk, waiting for a break in the traffic. At the first pause, we dashed halfway across the street to the island in the middle of the boulevard. After a couple of minutes on the soothing grass, we risked our lives again, dodging bicycles and cars to reach the fence. Too out of breath to talk, we dashed to the gap in the twisted wire to reach the sand on the other side. Daniel and I raced after Irko, our legs pumping across the scalding beach and into the salty waves.

This was Ostia in 1951, a city near Rome where my friends and I, our parents and many others like us lived in an old stone apartment building facing the sea. We came from different places. Irko, who was nine, from a place I could hardly pronounce: Czechoslovakia. Daniel came from Poland, and my parents and I from Romania, from a city called Chernowitz. Though we never talked about it, Daniel and I, both six years old, knew that Irko, like the grown-ups, had been in those places where almost everyone had died.

Our parents had made their way to Ostia where they tried to find a new destination that they could call home. Until they did, they filled their days sitting on the stone steps of our building, recalling the suffering they had been through. Irko, Daniel and I saw the tears in our parents' eyes and caught the familiar snatches of conversation, "taken in cattle cars…," "shot on the way to the railway station…," "hid in a barn for two years…," "I don't know where they are...." I felt a gnawing ache in my throat when I saw my mother cry and I knew, just as well as Irko and Daniel did, that this was the time to stay away.

Along with their memories came words of despair about whether they would ever join family or friends in a country that might welcome them. There was the constant fear that the doctors might find a problem with their health that would disqualify them from entering another country, like the spot they found on my mother's lung. And what then, if they couldn't go? What would become of their lives? And of their children. My friends and I heard their anguish, made worse by our inability to help.

Irko was fearless. When we got to the water, he swam out so far that we could see him only when he bobbed up between the waves. We were afraid to follow him, content to build castles and dig trenches on the shore. Sometimes the waves were too strong and our castles got washed away. Defeated, we raced into the water, splashing the brine into each other's faces until without warning, a wave grabbed our ankles and tipped us into the sea. Later, we made our way back home. With the sun setting behind us, we ran halfway across the street and waited as we'd done before for a chance to cross the rest of the way. Irko and Daniel saw a break in the traffic and ran ahead. I hesitated and checked the traffic again. Just then, I saw a police officer on a motorcycle coming toward me. He stopped, not caring about the cars behind him and asked me my name.

"Sammy," I replied, terrified of what else he might ask. I knew only a few words in his language. Would he take me away, like the people in the stories my parents told? Would I ever see my parents again? I started to cry.

"Where do you live?"

Between sobs I pointed to the building across the street.

"Why are you crying?" he asked. I wanted to stop crying. I didn't want him to think that I had done anything wrong. I couldn't think of an answer that wouldn't get me and my parents into trouble.

He looked around and when there was a lull in the traffic he told me to walk across the street. I was careful not to run. When I heard the roar of his engine, I knew I was free. I made sure that there were no tears on my face when I got back to our apartment. I didn't want my parents to know. My mother didn't notice and as always kept me at the door until she handed me a towel. As I reached for it, I sensed excitement in her voice and glanced toward my father at the kitchen table. It looked like he was working on a cardboard box, trying to open it. I stood rigid, staring in his direction, trying to figure out what was happening. It could be only one thing! A parcel from my brothers!

Forgetting everything that had happened, I raced into the bathroom and changed.

"It's a parcel from Leizer and Joe!" I shouted. My father didn't look up. Earnest, a kitchen knife in his hands, he carefully cut the carton open and pulled out the crumpled newspaper stuffed inside. My mother stared expectantly as my father took out the last of the paper and found an envelope resting on top of the neatly arranged boxes and tins. He raised the envelope and gazed at it for a moment before tearing off the edge. He read it aloud, in Yiddish.

Dear parents and Sammy,
We are, thank God, well.
It is now the middle of summer. The bitter cold of winter has been replaced by stifling heat. Harvest season is approaching. We will be working long hours with heavy machinery to bring in the crop of wheat.
We are sending you this parcel and hope you get it in time for Rosh Hashanah. We would like to send you more but it is all we can afford for now.
We hope that before long we will be together again.
With love and best wishes for a good new year!
Leizer and Joe

My father's voice broke slightly as he finished the letter and I found myself tearing up at the sight of my mother wiping her eyes. One by one, my father handed the tins and boxes to my mother: canned food, chocolate, all delicacies we couldn't afford to buy. I knew that my mother would make sure that they lasted a long time. Who knew when the next parcel would arrive? For now, though, she took out a chocolate bar and broke off a small square for each of us. I savoured mine, a crumb at a time, letting each morsel melt slowly on my tongue.

I longed for my brothers. When my mother took out the only picture of them that she had, I sat beside her and tried to look into it, deeply, imagining a day when we would be together. I couldn't understand very much but I recalled the bits and pieces of what my parents repeated every day.

The War broke out. The Russians retreated. The Germans and Romanians took over. My mother's father was murdered by Ukrainian neighbours. My father's sister was shot trying in vain to protect her parents. Chased from their home in Viznitz, my parents and brothers, along with so many others, were herded into cattle cars, forced to walk for miles, seeing others die along the way, until they arrived in the village of Shargorod, a ghetto in Transnistria. They were plagued by hunger and lice. Joe almost died of typhus. The horse-drawn wagons went door-to-door to gather the dead. They were kept alive by a Jewish family that gave them shelter in a tiny corner of their hut. Uncle Simcha died. For three years, they awaited their own deaths each and every day.

The Russian army liberated them. They couldn't go home because battles were still raging around the city of Viznitz. They found refuge in Chernowitz, where I was born. Later my brothers left to cross borders, mountains, in the night. To face unknown enemies, alone except for one another. They made their way to Italy like so many others, displaced, looking for a home.

I was still an infant then. I didn't understand and had no idea that they had left. Now they were in Canada working on a farm in a place called Hoffer, founded by our distant relatives. They were survivors, heroes. My brothers. They would bring us home.

***

I awoke to the sound of my parents' hushed voices. There was no need to be quiet, except that there was something about their faces that told me to be still. They told me it was Yom Kippur. Together we walked down the stairs to the lobby of the building where all the other families were gathering, the adults making their way to the single room at the side that had been set up for prayer. My mother explained that I would have to stay in the lobby with my friends while she and my father joined the other adults in the "synagogue." We were not allowed in. This was a memorial service for those who had perished, whose names would be recalled. The same names that I heard every day.

I watched as the adults crowded into the room. Men stood shoulder to shoulder in the doorway. The rabbi led the prayers, then suddenly he stopped. Everyone continued in private whispers. Minutes later he began a mournful chant. I didn't understand the words. I heard a sob. Faint. Then another. Louder. Chilling cries, bodies begging to collapse.

I strained to see my parents. I wanted them back. I was afraid. Angry. Why did this happen? Why did they grieve so much? Why was their pain so loud? Why me?

***

One day an official letter arrived. My father opened it carefully. It was from a government office. We were to come to Rome for a meeting about our application to go to Canada. From that moment on, my parents spoke of nothing else. Hour upon hour they debated all possibilities, all the questions my father might be asked by the officials. They had wanted this but now they were terrified.

I told my parents nothing of my own excitement. My first trip on a train!

My father wore the only suit he owned, my mother and I were dressed in the best we had. I sat beside her, next to the window, captivated by the scenery speeding by.

My mother leaned closer to me. "Remember, Sammy, when we get to the office, don't say anything, nothing at all. One wrong word and we won't be allowed to leave," she said for what felt like the hundredth time, in a whisper that sent chills up my spine. The more I heard these warnings, the more anxious I became that I might make a mistake and sink our chances. I thought of the close call I had had with the policeman on the motorcycle and shrank into my seat.

When we got to Rome, we made our way to a small government building. Once there, we walked up a flight of stairs where my father introduced himself to the receptionist and was told to proceed up another set of stairs to an office on the next level. My mother and I were asked to stay and wait for him to return.

My mother chose a chair from which she could watch the door to the office into which my father had gone. As time wore on, the suffocating heat felt even more stifling with the stillness of the room, broken up only by the clatter of the secretary's typewriter.

From time to time, people emerged from various offices upstairs and with expressionless faces left the building, some acknowledging the secretary on their way out. There were no toys, so I contented myself with leafing through the pictures in magazines, occasionally catching my mother gazing wearily my way. A creak in the floor above snatched our attention. The door opened and my father stepped onto the landing, his eyes immediately locking onto my mother's. The hint of a smile appeared behind his moustache. He seemed taller as he descended the stairs. At last he was with us.

Wrapping his arm around my mother's shoulders, he ushered her outside. I followed closely on their heels. They walked a few steps in silence. Then, his head held strangely back, my father said, "We can go." My mother, gripping my father's arm, laughed, repeating his name, "Dudel, Dudel..."

Overcome with joy, I heard myself proclaim, "So, Hoffer, you're going to Canada!"

First Encounters

I spent many hours at windows. First on a ship from Ostia to London and from there on a BOAC Stratocruiser that lifted us into the sky, its four massive propellers grinding their way across the vast waters below. Just when we lost sight of both land and sea, the airplane, as if it had lost its bearings, began to heave, falling without warning and then steadying itself, only to drop again. It went on forever. I looked at my father, hoping for reassurance, but he sat bewildered in his seat. My mother became violently ill. I was terrified that even if the airplane didn't crash, she might die.

None of us spoke a word of English so there was no way of asking what was happening. We stared at the hostesses in the aisle looking desperately for clues but they were themselves gripping the seats as they passed by, their faces expressionless.

After a time, the turbulence ended but we never felt calm again. Only the steady roar of the engines gave us some comfort that for the moment we were safe.

Many hours passed as we flew in the dark. Most people slept. Others seemed to gaze at their reflections in the windows. A surge of joy coursed through my veins when I saw far below us in the pitch black night, the flicker of tiny lights. Canada! My father said that these must be small towns. We watched as the clusters of light became larger and larger, until a vast expanse of stars spread out below us, a place my father called Montreal.

My parents' friends from Chernowitz, who had come to Montreal a year earlier, picked us up at the airport and took us to their apartment. Alye, telling my parents about another family from Chernowitz that lived nearby, said, "Let's ring them up..." I'd never heard that expression before and watched spellbound as he reached for the black instrument on the small table at his side, placed a horn-shaped part of it to his ear and, holding it there with one hand, turned a dial on the other part that was still on the table. When he finished turning the dial, he was silent for a moment and then began to talk. This was Montreal. This was Canada.

A couple of days later we set out for Winnipeg, where at last we would join my brothers. We travelled by train along tracks that wove their way through an endless forest. Was this what all of Canada was like? A tunnel through the woods?

When at last we arrived in Winnipeg, the train spilled us into a cavernous railway station. Our suitcases at our side, we scanned the crowds, the vast spaces. I stood there overcome with excitement but as the minutes passed and the crowd cleared, I saw in my parents' faces my fear that my brothers might not come at all.

When I saw two men emerge from a passageway, walking tall and determined, I knew it was them. "There they are!" I screamed. We ran toward each other. I was up in their arms, embracing, hugging, kissing, overcome with joy, disbelief and tears.

"Which one is which?" my father asked me, after a couple of minutes. My mother handed me the picture we had studied so many times before. I looked up at their faces. They were so much older now. Cautiously, I said, "This is this one and this is that one."

"But you know their names," my father chided, "tell us."

"This is Joe and this is Leizer," I pointed quickly.

"Right!" They all rejoiced

As we walked toward my brothers' hotel, I could hardly take my eyes off them, running along to keep up. From the conversation I learned that we wouldn't be staying here long. We were to leave the next morning on the journey to our final destination, the town of Hoffer.

In the afternoon, my brothers took me along to buy some gifts for our relatives. We went to a large store where I was overwhelmed by a flood of lights and colours and countless toys. I watched as they chose a pistol and holster set, silver metal guns with ivory coloured handles. And another set made out of brown plastic. I didn't ask why they bought guns but I did wonder. There was so much to choose from.

Back at the hotel, I removed one of the silver pistols from its holster. It fit perfectly in my hand. I tilted it to one side and released the chamber. It fell out easily on its hinges. Inside there were six smooth holes for bullets. I snapped the chamber shut and kept the pistol next to me.

Leizer stayed in Winnipeg, where he lived. The rest of us continued on by train with Joe. It was another endless trip, this time through lands that grew increasingly flat, only a cluster of trees here and there and tiny villages along the way. As the train rolled along, Joe told us of the challenges that he and Leizer had faced in the months and years after they had left us in the middle of the night.

They had made their way across Europe, with only coins in their pockets, facing untold danger. They crossed the Alps into Italy and reached Cremona where they joined hundreds of others, all waiting for a final destination. Many went from there to Israel. For him and Leizer, the choice was more complicated. They had learned that there was a Hoffer family that lived in a farming community in Canada, a country they knew nothing about. When a representative from Canada appeared at the relocation camp in Cremona, they made their decision.

When they arrived in Canada, they joined our distant relatives who had founded Hoffer, a hamlet on what we later learned were the Saskatchewan prairies. They embarked on a new life, working on the large Hoffer farm. The work was hard, the days long and the weather unforgiving. After a time, Leizer moved to Winnipeg. Joe said that he continued on the Hoffer farm, hoping that if we were all together again, we might establish a new life on a farm of our own. After years of waiting during which Joe had urged Mayer Hoffer, the patriarch of the family, to help bring us to Canada, he had taken things into his own hands. A visit to an immigration official in Winnipeg arranged through friends ended successfully and Joe was assured that our application would be approved.

Now, as the train took us ever closer to our destination, I could hear in their voices the gratitude that my parents felt to the Hoffers for having given my brothers a home. The tears that I had seen every day on the steps of our apartment building in Ostia had given way to smiles that I had never seen before. I felt again the warmth and excitement I had known in the railway station when I first saw my brothers. It was the feeling I had longed for when my mother and I had studied my brothers' picture, not knowing if we would ever see them. Now I felt special. I was one of them.

When at last we arrived in Hoffer, Murray and Rita, Mayer Hoffer's son and daughter-in-law welcomed us into their spacious home, flooded with light and things I had never seen before. They invited us into a large room with many seats. Reverently, my father and mother entered.

A man by the name of Avrum also greeted us. Joe had said that he was a relative of the Hoffers and had survived the concentration camps. He looked frail and ashen but appeared to have a wiry resilience about him. He and my parents exchanged only a few words, in Yiddish, communicating more by the looks in their eyes.

I followed the conversation, glancing now and then at the young boy whose name I didn't yet know, sitting on the floor, Murray and Rita's son. During the first lull in the conversation, I watched as Joe stood, saying, "Marshall, I have something for you that I got in Winnipeg." The boy looked up in anticipation as Joe carefully removed the holster from the bag and, smiling, offered Marshall the sparkling silver guns.

He gave the other ones to me.

By the Light of Day

I woke up to strange surroundings with vague memories of our arrival the night before. Images of a big bright house flashed before me followed by a twinge of pain at the memory of Joe giving away the beautiful guns to the Hoffers' son. I recalled getting into a car and being driven to a small house where we went to sleep.

As I rubbed my eyes, I heard the sound of my parents' voices coming from just outside the window above the couch I had slept on. Terrified that something was wrong, or even worse, that they might leave, I leapt into my clothes, just as they came back into the house.

My mother put her finger to her lips. She pointed to a closed door off the room and mouthed the word "Rabbi."

Relieved that my parents were back, I looked around more closely. There was a wood stove along one wall and, near it, a table with four chairs. Two doors led into other rooms. I faintly recalled my parents going into one of them the previous night, telling me in whispers before they went to bed that the rabbi was asleep in the other room.

In a whisper, my mother told me that she was going back to the Hoffers to see where Joe lived. Their house was just up the hill from where we were, Murray had told her. I could join her if I got ready quickly. My father, already preparing for his morning prayers, was not coming.

The Hoffers' house was at the top of the hill overlooking the town. Under the vast blue sky and drenched in warm sunlight, the few houses around us looked peacefully at rest. There were no people walking about. An empty road running along the edge of the town suggested a solitude bordering on loneliness. Only the two gigantic, narrow buildings that reached into the sky and proclaimed the town's name told me that there was a lot more about this place that I did not know.

As we approached the Hoffers' home, I caught sight of a large red building at the far end of the yard. It had a peaked roof that curved down the two sides of the structure, like a girl's hair enveloping her face. Beside the building and surrounded by a fence of posts and wire were some cattle slowly chewing hay, entirely uninterested in us. Along the way to the building stood a small wooden shack.

"That's probably where Joe is sleeping," my mother said. I ran toward the shack, alarming the chickens along the way. I waited at the door for my mother to knock. When she did, there was silence and then the muffled sound of steps approaching.

When Joe opened the door, it was hard to see inside. The morning sun didn't seem to penetrate the darkness. Joe stood, barefoot, squinting, his hand shading his eyes.

My mother peered in, behind him, straining to see. "You sleep here?" she asked. "In this straw? With those rags for blankets?"

Joe didn't answer, wiping the sleep from his face and adjusting his clothes.

My mother turned away, her trembling hands at her face. I took her elbow. "What's the matter, mom?" I asked, pained to see her like this.

"Come to the house when you're up," she managed to say.

"I can't," Joe replied. "I have to go to work."

Escape

The instructions in my workbook made no sense. The bold print said, "Complete the figures." There were no figures on the page, only numbers, mysteriously followed by blanks. Figures meant pictures of people or things. Even I knew that.

By now I had been going to school for a few weeks, in the one-room schoolhouse at the edge of town. Grade 1 wasn't hard as long as I understood what was being said by the teacher in the classroom and by the kids during recess or lunchtime. That was when the older kids tried out strange words on me that made them laugh and just got me mad. I answered them in the only language I knew, Yiddish. I used words that even I didn't know I knew.

I was six years old. Mrs. Miller had put me into Grade 1 because although I was a year older than the others, I had never gone to school. She was a kind teacher, nice to all of us in the single room that housed Grades 1 to 6. But when she tried to explain something to me, slowly, repeatedly, in the language I was still trying to understand, the whole school listened in.

If I didn't get this homework done, it meant another day of embarrassment and probably more teasing in the schoolyard. "I can swear that figures means shapes," I told my parents as they looked blankly at the page. "How," I asked, "can I complete drawings if there are no drawings to complete?"

After one last failed attempt, I screamed, "If learning English is going to be this hard, I'm going to live with the animals!" I jumped out of my chair and ran out the door. I crossed the dirt road that passed by our house and continued down into the ditch and through the grass that was as tall as me. I crossed the railway tracks and raced into the empty field. I kept running. I felt free, ready to go on forever.

I stopped for a moment, looked back and saw that no one was following me. The tall grain elevator buildings that stood guard over the town looked smaller now, the houses just tiny toys. I kept going through the empty field just trying to get farther and farther away. When I came to a barbed wire fence, I crawled under it, into a pasture. I had never been in a pasture before but knew that this was where the farmers' animals grazed. I saw no sign of cows or anything else and just kept going.

The ground was rougher now. The grass lay flat, some of it grey, some of it a sickly green. On the cultivated field the ground had been level and soft; now it was hard, dried out and hilly. When I ran down one of the slopes, I lost sight completely of the town and even the elevators. I was on my own.

As I came to the top of a small rise, I saw a farmhouse off in the distance. I had no idea who lived there but I decided to continue in that direction. At least it took me farther from my homework. Then, just as I descended into the next dip in the pasture, I was stopped, dead in my tracks, by the unmistakable scent of a skunk. Strong and close. I scanned the grass but saw nothing. Terrified, I turned back, running as fast as I could to escape the smell. My feet pumped tirelessly until I saw the familiar buildings of the village and our house.

I crossed the railway tracks, fought my way through the grass and went on over the road, not sure how I would explain why I had returned. I slowed down and stepped calmly into the house. My parents didn't look up from what they were doing. I searched their faces through the corner of my eye. They hardly noticed that I was there.

Exhausted, I sat down at the kitchen table. I glanced up as my parents' eyes met and drank deeply from my glass of fresh cold milk.

Home

We had just settled in to living in the little town of Hoffer when we got the news. We were going to leave the hut we were living in with the Rabbi and were moving to our own farm: a house, endless open fields, animals, big new machines, and all of us together. It was all that I could imagine.

I tried to ignore most of the things I heard Joe and my parents discuss about the farm not really being ours, that we were actually "renting" it from the "EKA," the JCA (Jewish Colonization Association). What I did grasp was that our farm was part of the Jewish community of farmers called the Sonnenfeld Colony. Even if the farm didn't belong to us, I thought, it was good enough for me. It didn't seem to bother my parents either, and Joe seemed to be happy. It was ours!

Our farm, Joe said, was five miles from Hoffer. My imagination soared when he told us that there were ninety people in Oungre, a town that was a short distance from our farm. And I was going to go to a big school there. Although it sounded exciting, I felt a pang of regret at the thought that I wouldn't be with the friends I had made in Hoffer. But Joe said that I would see the Jewish kids when the families in the colony got together.

When we finally drove into the yard and saw for the first time the sagging hut that would be our home, we were all perfectly silent. As we drove up to the house, I could see that its walls were made of long grey boards held together by nails that bled rusty stains. The roof sagged in the middle, looking tired and beaten, the window frames were rotten and splintered, some barely holding together cracked panes of glass. I wondered what my parents thought.

Inside, we found an empty room with a wood stove and two windows facing the road we had come on. The floors were covered in cracked, worn linoleum, the walls no colour at all. There were doors to two smaller rooms with beds made of brown painted metal frames and stained drooping mattresses. When my father lifted the end of one of the mattresses, we saw the rusty springs, almost touching the floor. Each bedroom had a window facing the fields behind the house. I wondered which bedroom I would sleep in but kept my questions to myself.

I was relieved to go outside. Joe pointed to the houses nestled in a cluster just across the fields, to the square white building near the edge of town that was going to be my school. It was as big as Joe had said, with many windows facing us and who knew how many on the other side. I wondered for a moment how I would get there and what the teachers and kids would be like.

I continued with Joe and my parents around the yard, listening. A tiny hut, just big enough for one person to go into, and three dilapidated shacks stood in a row. All were made of the same wooden boards as the house. They looked just as tired, barely holding each other up.

We started at the "outhouse," the farthest little building from the house. I had never used one of these before and wondered about having to go all that way every time I needed the bathroom. My parents wondered too. Joe assured us that he would move the outhouse closer and put it on the other side of the driveway opposite the house.

Next to the outhouse was a shed that stored tools, wire, blocks of wood, rope, screws, nails and countless other things that we might need some day. I just knew that this would be my favourite place, where I could explore the treasure that was piled on the floor and on the rickety shelves.

Beside the tool shed was the chicken coop where Joe said we would keep our chickens during the night. He would bring full-grown chickens in a few days, he said, but also eggs that we would keep in the house until they hatched. I was excited at the idea that chicks would actually come out of eggs, and wondered how they were different from the eggs that I had eaten all my life. I was thrilled that these chicks might become my pets.

The shack closest to our house was the granary. It was tiny. When I looked at the big field beside our house, that Joe said was our land, I was sure that there would be much more grain than this shed could hold.

One day, a month or so after we had moved in, a team of men arrived with a tractor pulling a pair of huge wooden poles on wheels. They drove into the yard of the farm next to ours where they carefully raised the abandoned house onto the poles. The tractor pulled the house very carefully into our yard then eased it down and attached it to the house we lived in. Our joy was written across my mother's face. Now we could move the stove into the new space. The big room in the first house could be for guests.

We had more space, but not much of anything else. We had no electricity and no phone. There was a phone in town, Joe said, in Durst's grocery store. We could use it. But we didn't really have anyone to call, except maybe in an emergency. Still, no one complained. We felt a kind of freedom in our own home that we had never felt before. And with Joe living with us, it felt, for the first time, as if we were a family, starting out on our new life.

War!

The greatest news after we arrived on the farm was that there was a boy my age who lived in town, just over the hill from our farm. His parents had arrived in the colony long before us. They had a farm that they actually owned and a fancy house that reminded me of my relatives' home in Hoffer. After I met Michael, we spent hardly a minute apart.

Going to Michael's house in Oungre was a treat for me. His house stood on a small hill overlooking the town. He lived a lot closer to our school than I did, and from his place we could see all the comings and goings down below.

Michael's father had dumped a large pile of sand right near the entrance to their house for Michael to play in. At one end of the pile, Michael had arranged his toys in a neat row: bulldozers, tractors, tanks, airplanes and guns.

One of our favourite games was conquering the Germans. Everyone said that the Germans had tried to kill all the Jews. Michael's parents had told him that too. It was our job to get revenge.

On a bright summer's day all was still, except for the roar of our engines. We dug in, using the heaviest machinery, to shape hills and build fortifications for our army and air force. Nearby, we set up the German bunkers, their machine guns and tanks.

Michael built his own model airplanes and was a master pilot. Wearing goggles, he came suddenly around the corner of the house, an airplane in his hand, diving at the enemy's tanks. He dropped his bombs. Boom! Boom! With each explosion, I smashed some of the German armaments. But their anti-aircraft guns were blazing, barely missing Michael's plane. He dove to escape, climbed to new heights and dove again, letting loose with his machine guns. Three more hits!

We attacked with our big Sherman tanks, bashing their positions to bits, knocking over their bunkers and killing their soldiers. We blasted the Germans wherever we saw them. Some were still shooting at us. Others were trying to get away.

Boom! "That's for the Jews you killed!"

"And for the ones you tortured!" Boom! Boom!

When we were finished with the tank battles, we hit them with rifles and bayonets. Hand-to-hand combat.

Just like in our comic books, the Germans didn't stand a chance.

Crops of Hope

Joe's singing echoed for miles around, above the din of the Massey 44 tractor. As he passed near the house, I watched the seeds drop from the cultivator in even rows, the spaces between them a measure of our hope for a plentiful crop. In the weeks that followed, the rains were few and the winds carried clouds of soil away. Somehow, miraculously, the seeds did not give up. Stiff green shoots sprouted, stretching their thirsty necks to the sky. In the weeks that followed, they found their adolescent strength, growing to new heights and proudly displaying heads of grain in an ever-thickening crop.

On a warm sunny afternoon, with hardly a cloud overhead, I caught a glimpse of lightning on the horizon and heard the soft rumble of thunder. Would it come our way? Would it be the rain we had been waiting for, or a deadly storm?

"Mom, it's going to rain," I announced as the mounting breeze carried me into the house.

"I can see," she replied. "It looks like there's going to be a lot of lightning."

"Go get the axe," my father said. Joe's knotted brow as he chewed his fingernails at the kitchen table told me to do just as I was told.

I took the axe from its place at the front door and went outside. The screen door slammed shut just as a piercing crack of thunder threatened to devour me. Quickly I set the axe on the highest spot in our driveway, anchoring its heel in the ground, the blade turned upward. My mother said that the axe would protect us from the lightning.

Low, billowing clouds in shades of black and grey churned across the menacing sky. Each gust of wind took my parents' nervous talk to the last remaining wedge of blue on the horizon, still visible from the kitchen window. Swirls of dust rose up in the yard, and in the fields the waves of grain were whipped by the gathering storm. Dirt blasted our walls. We were in the way.

In minutes there were flashes of lightening everywhere. Violent claps of thunder. Hail, driven by the wind. My mother held a pillow against the kitchen window to soften the blows of stones hurled from the sky. What would happen, I wondered, if the hail broke through?

When the storm finally passed, I followed my father and Joe toward the field behind the house. They didn't talk as they made their way through the vegetable garden, hailstones still melting on the ground. When we got there, our fears were confirmed. Among the few still-standing sheaves were many broken stems; others lay flat on the ground. Bending down to straighten one out, Joe said, "It's early, the crop might still recover."

Maybe it would. At least some.

Saturday Night

We didn't have a phone so the news got out in other ways: a chance encounter at the store in town, a word exchanged on a country road and messages carried home by friends at school. There was going to be a party at our house on Saturday night!

We were one of a handful of families, Holocaust survivors, who in the early '50s joined the Sonnenfeld Colony, a small Jewish farming community on the Saskatchewan prairies. Our home, like those of the other recent arrivals, was little more than a shack made of weathered boards held together by rust-stained nails, its windows single panes of glass that wobbled in their rotting frames. We had no electricity, no plumbing, an outhouse and only a wood stove to keep us from freezing in the cruel winter. My father drew our water from a well at the bottom of the hill on which our house stood. Pail in hand, he climbed through snowdrifts in the bitter cold and biting wind.

The challenges in summer were equally great. The stifling heat scorched the crops and conspired with the winds to propel clouds of grit into every crevice of our lives. Equally unyielding, however, was my mother's determination to make our house a source of pride, especially when we had guests.

Her ritual preparations began even before word of a party had escaped our lips. She inspected and cleaned every corner of the house, dusted the sofa and covered the worn-out seats with a fresh blanket, polished the wood stove, scrubbed the cracked linoleum floor and rearranged the few trinkets that we had, all the while singing her favourite songs from back home, before the War. Occasionally, she broke into a spirited polka, alone, with her broom.

My father gathered his copies of *The Forward*, the Yiddish newspaper that came to us all the way from New York, picking the stories that he would read to our guests. He collected the butts of the cigarettes he'd smoked all week, took them apart and spread the tobacco on rolling papers. Carefully, he shaped each prize, licked the edges of the papers and sealed them shut, adding to his supply for the approaching evening.

On Friday afternoon, well before sundown, my father took the hi-test lamp from its hook on the ceiling and filled it with fuel. He didn't light it yet. The coal oil lamp resting on the kitchen table, its glass chimney surrounding a modest wick, would be enough for us. Only on Saturday, after sundown, to the delight of everyone gathered in our house, would he light the hi-test lamp. The silken sacks that contained the flame would hiss and cast a brilliant light across the room.

Time had crawled by all week and slowed even more when the day finally arrived. As the sun crept lower in the sky, I stood watch on the driveway, willing every car and truck our way. I prayed that Harry and Mickey would come. They were the most fun when we played our favourite game, cops and robbers. But it was still too early. Impatient, I went to my dog, Boobie, chained at his rusty barrel under the cattle-loading chute. It was when he pulled his head from my arms, his ears alert, that I knew someone was coming. The pickup truck was still far away but, as always, Boobie somehow sensed that it was going to turn in. He went mad, barking, straining at his collar, desperate to break free. It was the Silvermans! I ran into the house to tell my parents and dashed out again, not to miss their arrival.

Harry was here! And then, a few minutes later, Mickey and Chucky arrived. There were four of us. Perfect for two teams.

We had no rules. Mostly it was just how well we hid, whatever game we were playing. When we discovered each other, we chased around the granaries and the house and between the cars and trucks in the yard. We didn't have toy weapons so we settled for shooting with our fingers and shouting, "You're dead!" only to hear, "I got you first!" Nobody won. But we made a lot of noise.

The sun had set but the growing darkness didn't slow us down. We ignored our mothers telling us that it was time to come in, instead playing harder, running faster and yelling louder, killing each other just one more time before the day was done. It was when we heard that final threatening call that we knew we had to stop. Unaware that the game was over, Harry came around the corner in a desperate dash, fell, tore his pants and scraped his knee. Bloody, he managed to get up and limp into the house, all of us right behind him, pleading that it wasn't our fault.

Harry's mother gathered him up and got some cold water on a towel. He screamed when she touched his knee. She tried to hush his cries, hoping that Harry's father would pay them no heed.

Sweaty and puffed out, the four of us settled on the floor in a corner of the room and read the few comic books I owned. My friends had seen them before and I worried that they might complain. But they didn't. Just like me, they enjoyed reading them over and over again.

The men, seated at the table, smoke wafting from their cigarettes, were totally absorbed in the only game they ever played, whist. They had paired up almost as soon as they had walked in the door, my brother Joe with Rachmiel and Marco with Moyshe. Between hands, they argued and teased.

"How could you throw away a ten of spades if you knew that the Queen was still out?"

"Who told you to bid three clubs? You didn't have the cards."

"Wait, we'll see who wins the next hand!"

The rumble went on until the last card was dealt, when they all fell silent.

My father's steady voice surfaced just then as he read a story from the newspaper folded in his hand. The women and couple of men around him listened, captivated by the recounting of personal experiences during and after the War. The spell was shattered when the last card was played and the voices erupted once again.

Halfway through the evening, my mother went into the kitchen to prepare the highlight of the party, "vursht sandwiches" made of salami and rye bread that came all the way from Winnipeg. My friends and I could have eaten everything up all by ourselves, but we knew better than to try. We were the last to be served. The men came first. It was the only interruption that they tolerated. Cake and tea finished off the meal. Still the card game carried on.

When my father finished reading, the people around him broke in with memories of their own horrors in ghettos and concentration camps. They told of what had happened to their families and friends in the short years since the War, things that they insisted were even more miraculous or disturbing than the stories my father had read – the rejoining of lovers, betrayal by friends, outrageous success, the hardships and disappointments of life in the New World.

After a time, with the salami gone and my father's stories read, the women began to make discreet suggestions to their husbands that the hour was late.

"Just a couple more hands," the men promised in a gaggle of voices.

Resigned, mothers found places for their sleeping children, on a bed, the couch or their own laps.

Much later, I awoke to the sounds of our guests leaving. Small children were bundled up in blankets. My friends, hardly able to stand, steadied themselves by leaning against their parents, their eyes closed. The adults shuffled to the door promising never again to let it get this late.

There was no argument. We had heard it all before.

The Chase

Boobie, like an arrow, streaked toward his target. Ears back, his grey fur pasted to his body, his legs a blur.

He raced after the rabbit that was trying desperately to escape. I stood, terrified that Boobie would catch it. I had visions of his long white fangs sinking into the rabbit's back. I screamed at him to stop. I knew that he could hear me but he was too taken with the challenge.

Boobie was gaining ground.

The open field offered the rabbit no hope.

Boobie was only inches behind when the rabbit reached the foot of the hill. My heart was in my throat. The rabbit started up the slope, its hind legs propelling it in arching hops that took it effortlessly up the hill. Boobie was suddenly falling behind. He pressed on, but the hill wasn't meant for him. He conceded defeat, his eyes following the rabbit where his legs wouldn't take him. He turned around, looking despondent, and loped back to me.

I put my arms around his head, scratched behind his ears and assured him that there would be another day.

Baseball Hero

I desperately wanted to be on the baseball team. But the truth is that I wasn't strong, I wasn't well coordinated and I was under the strictest orders from my mother not to get hurt. Even more important than not to come home with a broken arm or leg was not to break my glasses, which we couldn't afford to replace. When the ball was hit hard to me in left field, where I usually played, I got down on one knee, my glove open, to swallow the ball. I stayed there waiting, watching it tear through the grass. At the last second I turned my face away, just in time. I didn't get hit and my glasses didn't break. The ball whizzed by and the other team scored another run.

So I couldn't believe my luck when Mr. Knox announced that all the boys, including me, would be going to Tribune, the closest town, where we would play their grade sevens. When he read off our positions I wasn't surprised at not being in the starting lineup, but once again, he had me down for left field, if I got to play at all. Didn't Mr. Knox know that I would never be able to throw the ball in all the way from out there? But the good news was that I was on the team!

And I was on the bus! The one I never got to go on because, they said, our farm was only a mile from my school, too close to be picked up. As the bus roared by me every day, I envied my friends smiling and waving from the back window. But today I was one of them, sitting in the third row, beside Bruce, our second baseman. "We'll kill them," I screamed, even louder than the others. Tribune didn't stand a chance.

The bus came to a halt in the Tribune schoolyard. We could see the other team already out in the field, warming up. Mr. Knox ordered us to settle down and to get off without any pushing or shoving. He stepped off the bus. We piled out as fast as we could and unloaded our gear.

The Tribune coach called his team in. He walked over to Mr. Knox and shook hands. We huddled, shouted our team cheer and took to the field. Tribune was up to bat.

From the sidelines I urged the guys on through the first three scoreless innings. Then all hell broke loose. Top of the fourth, with Doug pitching. On the second pitch, their first baseman hit a triple. Their shortstop fouled out. Then the right fielder came up to bat. A stocky boy, he looked like he could hit. He was one of their favourites. Doug threw a beautiful strike. The kid swung with all his might but missed. He let the next one go by for a ball. Doug threw again. This time he connected, hitting the ball just over Bruce's head, for a single. Their first baseman ran home. One to nothing.

The next batter you could tell was a slugger.

"OK, Doug," Mr. Knox shouted. "You can do it, take your time." We cheered our support and watched Doug wind up.

"Have an eye, Gord," came the chorus from the other side. "Wait for a good one!" And he did. He waited and he walked.

With runners on first and second, we got very quiet. Their third baseman came up to bat. He had been watching Doug carefully. He looked like he batted with his head not his heart.

"Strike one!" the umpire called.

Looking at Paul behind home plate, Doug launched the ball again. It was going to catch the outside corner. The batter braced himself, tightened his grip and swung. The crack could be heard a mile away. The ball soared into the sky, on and on, finally landing far past Dennis, our right fielder. They all ran as soon as he hit the ball, urged on by the screaming of their classmates. A home run! Four to nothing.

Thanks to Bruce and Richard, our third baseman, we scored a run in the bottom of the fourth. Nowhere near what we needed to catch up, with three innings to go.

I got tired of watching Doug struggle and began to throw the ball to Donny, our backup catcher. Now and then I dropped a hint just loud enough for Mr. Knox to hear that maybe I should do the pitching.

If Mr. Knox heard me he didn't let on and kept encouraging Doug and the team. I persisted, throwing the ball seriously now and making sly remarks to catch Mr. Knox's ear.

Tribune got a few more on base but they didn't score another run after the blowout inning. Our guys seemed to have forgotten how to hit. Well, almost. Paul did hit Bruce to third in the bottom of the fifth, but that was all. The game was as good as lost.

Top of the seventh. I was sure that I was throwing the ball to Donny every bit as well as Doug was pitching. I glanced at Mr. Knox just as he looked my way. He pointed at me to go to the mound. I looked at him in disbelief, my first thought being whether I had upset him. Had I been too loud, too pushy? Or did he mean that I should go out to left field? No, he wanted me to pitch. Doug was already coming in. With a sinking feeling it occurred to me that I had no choice.

I got to the mound and looked at Paul. My God! He was a mile away. This wasn't what I had in mind. I was expected to throw some warm-up pitches. All eyes were on me. I was my team's last hope. But they had never seen me pitch before. I had never pitched before!

Suddenly I felt exhausted from all the ball tossing I'd done. But there was nowhere to hide, so I took aim at Paul's mitt. The ball barely made it across home plate. Paul tossed it back saying, "It's OK, Dave, just a little harder." He glanced at the other team's bench. They just sat there, grinning.

I threw again, this time with all my might. The ball took off and sailed three feet to the right of Paul's glove. He leapt to stop it but couldn't reach that far. He jogged to the wire screen behind him and threw the ball back to me, mouthing the words, "What's wrong?" My first batter. I wound up slowly, delaying as long as I could. I took one last glance at the menacing face at the plate and let go. He smashed the ball. A home run! The Tribune team went nuts.

There were no more home runs. A line drive to John at short for one out and then I walked the next four batters. I could see Paul cursing under his breath, as he reached wildly in all directions to catch my pitches. I tried desperately to get Mr. Knox to call me in but he just kept encouraging all of us. My classmates, watching from the sidelines, had grown painfully silent.

Then I got lucky. One infield fly that was easily caught by Rob at first, followed by a pop-up foul. Paul tossed his mask and took a few steps back. He caught the ball and I was home free!

There were no miracles in the bottom of the seventh. Humiliated, we gathered our stuff and got on the bus. No one looked my way or talked to me. Even Bruce said nothing. Mr. Knox was up at the front with the driver. He had hardly noticed me get on.

It was a long ride home.

A New Lasso

I discovered it by accident. Joe had said nothing about buying a new lasso but when I opened the door to the tool shed, there it was, magically deposited on a hook on the wall. Even in the dim light it was beautiful. Bright, gold, all coiled tightly together, it looked like a trophy in the middle of the mess of rusty tools and other scraps. I wanted to touch it but knew that if it dropped or unravelled, I would be as good as dead.

That afternoon, Chucky and Harry and their parents came to visit. Still excited about my discovery, I immediately led my friends to the shed. Before I could say a word, Harry dove in, grabbed the lasso off its hook and hoisted it onto his shoulder. They didn't pay any attention to my objections as they raced off to the corral.

Chucky opened the gate and we all stepped inside where the ground was a mess of thawed manure and puddles of half-melted snow. Harry lost no time to make a noose, his eye already fixed on a calf standing apart from the other cattle, watching us. He crept closer to the calf, swung the noose over his head and let it go. The lasso glistened in the sun as it arched through the air then fell smack into the slop. My heart sank with it but there was nothing I could do.

Harry gathered up the lasso, ignoring the stinking muck on the rope and got ready to do it over again. He edged closer, balancing himself on a couple of patches of snow and launched the noose. It hit the calf on the side of the neck. The calf didn't move.

More determined than ever, Harry got ready to try again. Chucky told him to throw it higher this time. He wound up and threw the noose. It sailed up into the air then dropped right over the calf's head and around its neck. Hardly believing what we saw, Chucky and I screamed at Harry to pull the rope tight and hold on.

Shocked, the calf leapt into the air, kicking and twisting. It took off, racing around the corral, yanking Harry off his feet and dragging him on his stomach through the pools of slush. We stopped screaming and finally, half way around the corral fence, Harry let go of the rope. As soon as it was free, the calf stopped dead in its tracks and just stared at us, steam jetting from its nostrils.

Harry got up slowly, not bothering to brush the mess off. He was soaked. As we started on our way to the well to clean him up, I glanced back at the calf. The noose was still around its neck, the rest of the lasso dangling on the ground. Joe would have to get it off. I was as good as dead.

Hunting Gophers

I didn't mind gophers, scurrying around the granaries or rearing up on their hind legs to check for danger.

But hunting them was fun.

It was another bright summer day. As I glanced at the field behind our house, I saw the golden shape of a gopher racing through stubble. It was all the prompting I needed. I got the gopher trap and a stick from the tool shed, filled a pail of water at the well and carried my gear into the field.

In minutes, I came across a small hole in the ground surrounded by a ring of soil, deposited there when the gopher had dug his tunnel.

I stepped on the foot pedal of the trap and separated the deadly metal teeth with my hands. I rested the trap carefully in the mouth of the hole, where I hoped the gopher would try to escape. Then, cautiously, I stretched the chain dangling from the end of the trap as far from the hole as I could, poked a stick through the ring at the end of the chain and with a rock, drove one end of the stick into the ground. I tugged on the chain to make sure that the stick wouldn't let go if the gopher tried to take off with the trap.

Slowly, I poured a steady stream of water down the hole, trying not to waste a drop and backed away.

From a distance, I saw a gopher emerge from another hole a short distance away, race across the field and disappear.

He had outsmarted me. But not for long.

Our .22 rifle sat on a shelf just inside the entrance to our house. I loaded the gun and made my way back to the field, taking a few extra bullets just in case.

Feeling like a soldier, I lay down on my stomach and took aim at the gopher hole. I waited. The gopher had no reason to come out. Patiently, I checked my sights.

At last I saw some movement. Just a hint. The gopher poked its nose out, enough to sniff the air. Then, up came its head. And shoulders. It stood on its hind legs. A bit braver now but alert. Surveying its surroundings.

A perfect target. I squeezed the trigger gently. I felt the rifle fire. The gopher disappeared.

Dead or alive? I would never know.

Mr. Diefenbaker's Visit

You could feel the excitement in the air. John Diefenbaker was coming.

I didn't know anything about him. Only that he was an important politician.

Joe and I joined everyone else from the farms and from the nearby towns at "the grove," a mile up the road from where we lived. The grove was a small collection of trees that had been planted many years before. It offered refreshing shade on the days when the school had its "field day" or the community gathered for a special event. Today, it wasn't the baseball field but the gazebo that was the centre of attention.

People sat in neat rows on the freshly cut lawn at the foot of the stand, listening intently.

Mr. Diefenbaker's white hair stirred slightly in the breeze. His jowls shook as his voice, in unison with his finger, punctuated his speech.

Only the rustle of the leaves, the birds flitting by and the occasional sound of a car on the highway coloured the tranquil afternoon.

I peeked out from behind the concession stand, a short distance from the gathering.

Mr. Diefenbaker's finger was poking the air with extra energy, his voice rising, just like on the radio. He paused. Everyone applauded.

Except me. I couldn't contain the urge. I heard myself shout, my hands cupped firmly around my mouth, "Booooo! Booooo!"

All heads turned. Hundreds of eyes glared at me. Worst of all, Mr. Diefenbaker's piercing stare found me, a frozen scowl on his face.

Helplessly, I stared back, my hands shrinking slowly to my sides.

I wanted desperately to disappear into thin air but was unable to move. What had I done wrong? That's what they did on the radio.

A Lesson

The old granary was just too small for the harvest we were expecting. Joe decided that we needed a new one, large enough to hold a whole crop of wheat.

He hired a carpenter who came with a couple of helpers. I watched them every day. First, planning with Joe where the building would go, then pouring the concrete, making the frame and nailing on the brand new pale yellow boards.

The men were on the roof, setting the shingles into place. I watched from a distance as they arranged the thin, wedge-shaped pieces of wood in a pattern, one overlapping the other so that the rain couldn't slip underneath. The men moved around carefully but easily, not bothered by the angle of the roof. I wondered how they could be so relaxed. One slip would have meant disaster.

When they were almost out of shingles, the carpenter came down the ladder to unpack another bundle. He was not in a hurry. When he got to the bottom, he stepped away from the ladder and took a deep breath, arching his back and stretching his arms to the sky. He reached into his carpenter's apron and fished out a pack of Players. He lit a cigarette, inhaling deeply and blew out the smoke. It was only then that he noticed me watching.

"Come here Sammy, I want to show you something," he beckoned.

I eagerly accepted the invitation. As I approached, he drew a shingle from the new bundle and held it up, pointing at the brown stains on the wood.

"Do you know what these are?" he asked.

"No," I said. But I had wondered.

"It's Jap blood," he answered with a grin, the cigarette dangling from between his teeth.

I stared at the shingle. The other shingles looked like that too. I remembered my comic books, American soldiers fighting the Japanese.

I watched the carpenter climb back up the ladder.

Could it be true?

The Truth

Visitors from outside the colony were as rare as movie stars. So when Joe walked into the house and dropped the mail on the kitchen table saying that Sonia and Hershel were coming, time stood still. My father reached for the open envelope among the newspapers.

"When are they coming?" my mother asked, beaming with anticipation. My father looked for the answer in the finely written Yiddish.

"In two weeks. And they're going to stay for about a week," Joe explained. "Hershel is recovering from his heart attack. They think it'll be good for him to take a rest."

"But they're driving so far...," my mother began. We all knew that Winnipeg was an eternity away.

"He'll be OK," Joe interrupted. My parents did not look convinced.

Hershel had been here the previous summer, before he got sick. I lit a firecracker and set it off just when he stepped out of the house onto the weathered wooden boards that served as our porch. As it sailed through the air, I wanted to grab it back but it was too late. I ducked around the corner of the house so he wouldn't see me but I knew he'd guess I did it. I couldn't tell if the bang scared him because he didn't say a word.

I called them "Uncle Hershel" and "Aunty Sonia" even though they weren't really. But they were like family to us. I had heard my brothers...

We lived with them when we came to Winnipeg after our first winter on the Hoffers' farm.

Their home was a gathering place for the Jewish boys who had just arrived from Europe, orphans after the Holocaust.

Sonia embraced us and our friends with the Yiddish of home and a welcoming table. No one needed an invitation. She was like a mother to us all.

Hershel was torn between what he'd learned at the yeshiva in Russia and the ideal world that the Russian Revolution had promised. But he was one of us. Eager, in his way, to be a father and friend.

It was Friday afternoon. My parents were preparing for Shabbos. My mother, who was never satisfied with the look of the house, the location of every trinket and the shine of every surface, made another of her countless rounds, checking and rechecking. Our house was little more than a shack, made of loosely fitted, weathered boards that let in the Prairie dust in summer and the snow in winter. Despite our primitive surroundings, my mother was undaunted. The house had to shine. Sonia and Hershel were special.

I remembered Sonia from the time she and Hershel visited us over two years earlier. Sonia was a chubby woman with a bright round face and grey hair. She was feisty and funny and brought with her a burst of energy that my mother longed for.

Hershel's grey hair gave him a wizened look. He was quick witted, with a twinkle in his eye that made you wonder what he was thinking. He respected my father's seriousness but maybe because he travelled so much, he was more modern in his outlook. The discussions gave my father a rare chance to come alive outside the newspapers that were his only escape. As the day wore on, I wondered impatiently how close they might be. None of us said a word, afraid to jinx their arrival.

Finally, to Boobie's trumpeting bark they pulled into the driveway. We rushed outside, watching them drive up and stop beside the house. Kisses, exclamations of joy when Hershel and Sonia and my parents embraced each other. The excitement continued as Hershel maneuvered to the back of the station wagon and opened the door, revealing bags of fresh rye bread, salami and other treats.

My father and Joe took most of the bags, Sonia and my mother brought the rest. Their hands full, they trooped single file into the house, letting the screen door slam shut behind them. Hershel remained outside, relishing the fresh air and casting off the strain of the long drive.

"How do you feel, Uncle Hershel?" I asked.

"Fine, Sammy, I feel fine," he replied, smiling generously. He opened the tailgate of the car again and reached for one of the suitcases. He removed a neatly packaged bundle and handed it to me – a whole set of comic books!

"Wow! Thanks!" I took them eagerly from his outstretched hand and stared at the covers: Superman, Donald Duck and Roy Rogers! I didn't allow myself to look inside. Not yet.

"Sonia, you sit," my mother insisted when dinner was over. "I'm going to clear off the dishes and wash them later. You stay in the living room and relax with the men."

"Not a chance, Sally. I didn't come here to be catered to," she replied, already out of her chair, removing a stray strand of grey hair from her face and gathering a set of empty plates.

My mother wrapped her arm around Sonia and kissed her on the cheek. "Sonia, I'm so glad you're here."

My father, Joe and Hershel continued their conversation at the living room table, drawing on their cigarettes. I didn't understand much of what they said but I relished the words, the gestures, the intensity of their talk. I didn't see this very often. It was exciting just to be there.

"It's the system." Joe argued, his voice raised to make his point. "They have a different system!"

"I don't disagree, Joe. But if you have money you can get an education in America too. Still, it's true, you have to have money," Hershel said.

"That's what I mean," Joe continued, leaning into Hershel's face, "I remember when we were in Viznitz and the Russians came into Romania before the War. The whole school system changed overnight. The Russians were interested in one thing – to get the best out of the students.

"But it's a godless society," my father interjected.

"What does God have to do with it?" Joe asked. "It's not about God, it's about people!" he insisted, loud enough to discourage my father from replying.

Hershel was suddenly quiet.

"Hershel," Joe continued after a moment's silence, his voice subdued but emphatic, his forehead knotted in concentration, "I want to know one thing. Which system will produce a better person?"

Hershel looked at Joe, considering the question. He glanced at my father who was sitting in his chair, gazing at the floor, but said nothing.

Did Hershel know the truth?

The Ten Commandments

I usually knew what the next movie in town was going to be from what the kids in town said at school, but this time it was Joe who announced that *The Ten Commandments* was going to be playing the following week.

"Really, Joe?" my mother replied. "They made a movie of the Ten Commandments?" We'll have to see it," she said, glancing at my father who was engrossed in his Yiddish newspaper at the kitchen table.

"I'd like to go," I said, also looking at my father.

"Dad, you should come too," Joe ventured, knowing that he resisted anything new.

"We'll see," he replied. My mother and Joe exchanged looks. My heart raced at the thought that my father might actually go. I wanted desperately to watch the look on his face when he saw the whole story of the Exodus from Egypt really happen.

The next day was Shabbos. As always, he called me to join him, opening the chumash, the Five Books of Moses, at the point where we had left off. I liked the stories and wanted to believe that they were true.

But today I had the movie on my mind. I wanted my father to come and decided that it would help if I paid close attention to his teaching. When we read about the snake tricking Eve into eating the apple, I asked, "Why did God allow the snake to do that?" I could see that he was pleased with my question so I went on, "Dad, are you going to come with us?"

After a moment he replied, "If you promise to study hard and practice your prayers, I'll go."

"I will, Dad, I promise," I answered.

"OK. That's enough for today," he said and returned to his studies.

The day finally arrived. After supper we all crowded into the truck with Joe behind the wheel, and drove into town. There were many more cars than usual parked in front of the town hall, a sure sign that the movie was a hit. I had heard on the radio that it had cost millions to make. More than any other movie, ever. I couldn't wait to see the parting of the Red Sea. And the burning bush. I wondered how they would do God. It had to be good for my father's sake.

We got there a little too close to movie time so my father didn't have a chance to smoke a cigarette. We went right into the hall and took our seats, my father at the aisle. At last the lights went out and we heard the whirring of the projector behind us. The screen flickered and then, the news of the world. A cartoon followed. This was always my favourite part but today I couldn't pay attention. I worried that my father would hate it. I looked over to him trying to read his expression in the dark. If he thought that the movie was going to be a cartoon, then God help us all.

Finally, the movie began. The deep voice of the narrator, the stirring music, a multitude of slaves toiling under the whips of taskmasters.

Not a sound was heard from the people around us as Pharaoh, Moses and Ramses appeared. I heard only my father in a low voice asking Joe who the characters were.

A few minutes later I heard a stirring to my left. I looked over and saw my father getting out of his seat and stepping into the aisle.

"Where are you going?" Joe whispered.

"This isn't Moses and it isn't Pharaoh. The whole thing is made up," my father replied. With one hand searching frantically for his cigarettes, he walked toward the exit.

There was nothing I could do. If only he would have stayed a little while longer and given the movie a chance, he might have understood. Maybe if it had been in Yiddish.

Tormented

Going to a movie in the city was a very special treat. And this time, my brothers invited me along! Just the three of us! They didn't say anything about the movie. I had no idea what it was about and I didn't care. Just going was enough.

It seemed to take us forever to get to Weyburn, although it was only a half-hour away from our farm. I watched out the car window for the signs marking the names of the villages so I could gauge how close we were, but I could never remember the order of the towns and I didn't want to ask. At last, I saw the familiar water tower on top of a distant hill. Slowly, the tower got bigger until I could actually make out "WEYBURN" printed near the top.

We drove up 3rd Street, parked the car and approached the theatre. Joe and Leizer walked quickly, drawing hard on their cigarettes. I raced along beside them, not saying a word.

When we stepped into the theatre, I was disappointed to see that there was hardly anybody there. But then I remembered that it was early afternoon and that people who lived here could come to see a movie any time. Not like in Oungre, where they played only on movie night.

There were no cartoons. The movie began. A young woman got into serious trouble with the law. She kept getting into more trouble even in jail but it wasn't always her fault. And then, they sentenced her to death. She was going to be killed!

I felt anxious, nervous. I looked around. There were no other kids in the theatre. There was nowhere I could go.

They led her into a room where she was strapped into a special chair. A minute passed, maybe two and then I saw what looked like thin white smoke rising from under the chair. When it got to her face she jerked her head up, trying not to breathe. She squirmed one way and then the other but the straps held tight. She struggled for a very long time, her face tortured.

I felt sick, unable to watch, but I couldn't look away. Finally, she stopped. I had never seen anyone die before.

The lights in the theatre came on. My brothers got up to leave. As we walked outside, I glanced at the poster. I didn't want ever to forget the name of this movie. I never wanted to see it again. It was called *I Want to Live.*

Outside, I walked behind my brothers. I heard Leizer say, "And that's how they were killed."

Instantly, I knew that he meant ... the gas chambers.

I keep my anguish to myself.

An Echo

Joe walked through the garden and into the field behind the house. He broke off a couple of heads of wheat from their sheaves and ground them up in the palm of his hand. From the window at our plastic-covered kitchen table, I squinted to see his reaction as he examined the seeds closely. Moments later he came back in, telling my father that the crop was almost ripe. There was no time to waste. In a couple of weeks harvesting would begin. The hay had to be brought in.

My father couldn't help. He had been weakened by all that he had lived through and was unacquainted with farm machinery. But haying wasn't a job for one person. Someone had to drive while the other lifted the bales onto the back of the truck. It was late in the season. This year, Joe said, he would need two men.

He had talked to Joey and asked if he could give him a hand for a couple of days. Joey had readily agreed. His father owned only a few cattle so he didn't have much haying to do. Besides, it was a chance for Joey to make some money before school started. For his second helper he asked Mr. Thomson, in town, if his son Peter was available. Peter had agreed to start early on Monday morning.

"Do you want to come with us tomorrow?" Joe asked me at supper on Sunday.

"Are you sure, Joe?" my mother interjected. "Will it be safe?

Exchanging glances with my father at the kitchen table, Joe said, "He'll be OK, it's time he did a day's work." My father didn't reply. He was not a man of many words. His silence was enough.

I couldn't sleep that night, imagining what the next day would be like, working with the men. I had no idea what I would have to do. I imagined myself throwing bales of hay onto the truck, though I knew that I could barely lift one off the ground.

I awoke at the first hint of dawn and got dressed quickly, quietly, hoping not to disturb anyone, especially Joe who might just change his mind if I woke him up. I slipped outside to Boobie who was always awake and eager to see me. I walked over to him and buried my face in his neck.

I heard the door open behind me and saw Joe coming outside.

"You're up," he said.

I prayed that he would remember what he'd said the night before. I wasn't about to remind him, so I just answered plainly, "I wanted to be ready to go."

Looking at his watch, Joe said, "Joey should be here soon and Peter will be walking from town. Go eat your breakfast because we're going to leave in half an hour."

I ran into the house, thrilled that Joe remembered.

"I saw you outside when I got up," my mother told me, assuring me that I had never been out of her sight. "You'd better eat a good breakfast. And I'll give you a sandwich to take along just in case you get hungry."

She cracked two eggs into the buttered frying pan on our wood stove, the sizzle instantly filling the kitchen with an aroma that made my mouth water. This was my favourite and only breakfast, fried eggs and the soft richly buttered challah that my mother baked, the golden crust crumbling in my mouth.

"What are you going to make for lunch?" I asked.

"I'm going to get some beets and potatoes from the garden and make a borsht. Would you like that?"

"Sure, but make it hot, mom, it's only good hot," I said, anticipating the sweet ruby red soup. Just then I heard Boobie barking. As I gulped down my glass of milk and ran outside, Joey pulled up to the house in his pickup truck.

Climbing out, he said, "Hey Sammy, you're up early."

"I'm going with you to help with the haying," I answered.

"Great," Joey replied, as he joined Joe at the stack of bales left over from last year.

"Good morning, Joey. Did you see Peter on your way?" Joe asked.

"No. Do you want me to go into town and pick him up?" Joey offered.

"No," Joe replied, "it's OK. It's still a bit early. If he doesn't show up soon, we'll all go and get him on the way to the slough. In the meantime, Joey, give me a hand with these bales so we can make room for the next load."

Joey grabbed each bale by the twine that held it together and tossed it effortlessly up to Joe who arranged the bales in a pyramid. Joey was only three years older than me but he was stocky and strong. He was no stranger to hard work, doing the planting and harvesting on his father's farm and caring for the animals.

Boobie's barking got our attention. Peter was walking up the driveway. I recognized him from the couple of times I had seen him in town.

"Peter, what's cookin'?" Joe asked as he approached the hay stack.

"Not much, Joe. Can I give you guys a hand?"

"No, I want to get going," Joe replied as he climbed down. We'll do this later. Let's get in the truck." Then turning to me he said, "You get in the back. I want you to sit down right behind the cab and stay there. Don't get up until we get to the slough." His stern voice made it clear that I would have a one and only chance to prove that I could be trusted. There was no way that I was going to so much as stir.

We travelled for miles along the gravel highway. I surveyed the receding fields, recognizing some of the farms where my friends lived. They were too far away for me to walk to and with the cost of gas I saw them only at house parties. But none of that mattered now.

Suddenly the truck slowed. I braced myself as we turned. I couldn't see what was ahead of us but I could feel the truck descending sharply. After a couple of minutes it levelled off and started to bounce from side to side. I knew that we were on the rough soil of the slough. Joe stopped the truck and we all got out.

"OK, Joey has an idea," Joe announced, looking at me. "He says that you should learn how to drive the truck. You'll drive and we'll throw the bales into the back. So, get in the cab and I'll show you what to do."

I couldn't believe my ears. Suddenly the idea of working with the men scared me. I wasn't ready for this. What if I wrecked the truck or ran into somebody? I wanted to tell Joe that I was still three years away from getting my driver's license. Why did I have to do this now? And in front of everybody? But I couldn't refuse. I would never live it down.

Reluctantly, I climbed into the cab. I had often imagined what it would be like to be able to jump into the truck and drive off, free as a bird. Now, ready or not, I wasn't imagining. This was the real thing!

Thankfully the motor was still running so I didn't have to start the truck. But what next?

"Now pay attention," Joe said. "Do you see the two pedals on the floor? With your left foot push down on the one on the left and keep it there. That's the clutch. Pull the gear shift into first gear, right here. Now all you have to do is let the clutch come up slowly while you press gently on the gas with your other foot and the truck will go forward. When you get to a set of bales I'll signal you to stop. That's when you'll take your foot off the gas, press down on the clutch again with your left foot, push on the brake with your other foot and move the gear shift up to neutral and take both feet off the pedals. Then I'll tell you when to move again."

I couldn't remember a thing that Joe had said. And there stood Joey and Peter, both grinning and, I was sure, waiting for me to fail.

No way was I going to let them make fun of me! I reached for the gear shift, pushed the clutch down and found first gear. I let the clutch up slowly. Now the gas. I pressed lightly. The clutch was up all the way but nothing happened. I gave it more gas. The motor revved up but still the truck didn't move. I pressed the gas pedal down all the way. The truck took off like a bronco, bouncing wildly over clumps of soil. With my foot still on the gas pedal, the truck raced toward the bales. I slammed on the brake. The truck came to a violent halt and conked out.

Joey was holding his stomach, roaring with laughter. Joe seemed to think it was funny too. Only Peter who'd been grinning a minute earlier didn't laugh.

"Peter, do me favour," Joe said. "Jump in the cab beside Sammy and help him get going. We'll meet you at the bales over there."

Peter got into the cab. I was glad that he didn't start lecturing me. I knew that I had pushed too hard on the pedal and then didn't lighten up when the truck started moving. But how do you manage that if you're driving over lumps and bumps?

"Here's what we'll do, Sammy," Peter began. "Just take it a step at a time and we'll get there. It's OK. Don't tell them, but the first time I drove, I tried to show my father that I could back up and ran right into our garage door."

Peter coached me to the next set of bales where he jumped out to help Joey toss them onto the truck while Joe arranged them in rows to build a neat, sturdy pile. He did it again at the next set of bales. By the third set, I had gotten the hang of it and caught Peter smiling. I smiled back, biting my lip as I did it for the first time by myself.

It was almost noon. We got ready to go home.

"OK, Sammy, you did a good job," Joe said, Joey and Peter nodding in agreement. "Now you go up in the back and sit in the space I made for you just behind the cab, between the bales. You'll be safe there. Nothing will tip over on you but you'll have to stay still, where Joey can keep an eye on you through the back window.

I climbed up and settled in, inhaling the sweet smell of the hay. On the way back, too low to see anything, I relived the morning, detail by detail, overflowing with pride. I could drive!

In the yard, Joe backed the truck up to the hay stack. He decided not to unload the bales just yet. "Tell mom we're here," he said. "We'll come in as soon as we wash up at the well."

When they came into the kitchen, everything was ready at the table. "It smells great in here," Joe proclaimed. We took our seats, Joe not losing a minute to dive into the freshly baked bread. The others followed. I took my piece last.

"What about dad?" I asked.

"He's already eaten," my mother replied. "He's out in the garden doing some weeding."

With the men devouring the bread, my mother took Joe's soup bowl and filled it at the stove with her favourite steaming beet borsht and brought it to the table. She did the same for Joey. Eagerly, they ladled the soup into their mouths.

My mother filled Peter's bowl next and placed it in front of him. He stared at the soup, not lifting his spoon.

Joe noticed and asked, "Peter, why aren't you eating?"

Still staring at the steaming bowl, Peter replied, "It looks like blood."

My mother gasped as she covered her mouth.

Dead silence. Then Joe replied, in a quiet voice I had never heard before, "It's beets, Peter."

Peter didn't stir. My mother removed his dish.

There was no table chatter after that, just eating in silence. Peter ate too. Not another word was said about the soup.

Everyone was relieved when, finally, Joe pushed his chair away from the table, declaring, "To rest is not to conquer." They unloaded the truck and left to get another load of hay.

When the men left the kitchen, my mother sat down, pale and shaken. Not knowing what else to say or do, I brought her a glass of water. "Why did Peter say that?" I asked her.

She didn't answer. She started to cry, just as my father came in.

"What happened?" he asked, looking at me. "Why is mom upset?" He glanced outside, to see if Joe was still there.

Through her tears she said, "Dudel, the boy said that the borsht was blood. Nothing has changed, Dudel. They still think we are murderers."

My father sat down in stone-faced silence.

"He'll tell everyone," she added, wiping the tears from her face, "and they'll all believe him."

Survival

Becoming citizens of Canada was a big deal. It had taken five years but at last, in the middle of winter, Leizer and Joe were to make the trip to Estevan, a small city less than an hour away, to get "the papers" that would make them officially Canadian. It was not something that could be rescheduled or missed. They dressed in their finest and left early in the morning to avoid the oncoming winter storm.

The bright sunshine and stillness suggested that the storm might pass us by but my father spread extra hay in the corral for the cattle, just in case. He carried pails of water up the hill from the well and topped up the water tank. The cattle attacked the hay, all straining for their share.

The chickens took no notice of the clouds moving in or of the occasional gust of wind. They pecked happily at the crumbs my mother had scattered on the ground. Now, seeing the change in the weather, she rounded them up and chased them into the safety of the chicken coop.

Boobie seemed to sense that something was up. On his chain, he paced back and forth in front of his dog house, occasionally raising his head to sniff the air. I went over to him and scratched behind his ears, checking that he'd emptied his bowl of bread and milk.

Over lunch my mother asked, "Dudel, do you think they're there yet?"

"I'm sure they're there by now," he replied, though I could tell that he shared my mother's fears.

Had the storm already hit where they were, I wondered. Could they be stuck somewhere on the road?

Secretly, I hoped that Daryl, our hired man, would stay with us overnight, though I knew that, as always, he would be going home by supper time.

The wind grew stronger whipping up swirls of snow. The sun, a shrunken ball of white, drifted in and out of the menacing clouds. Even as I watched, the sky darkened, the clouds growing thicker and blocking out what was left of the afternoon light. I glanced at Boobie. He was resting on the loose hay inside his barrel, protected from the wind.

Night came early. Daryl had gone home. My father lit the coal oil lamp on the kitchen table, the flickering flame assuring us that the breeze we felt in the house was real. The rattle of a loose board, the whine of the wind caught in some unknown crevice, the draft that sucked the warm air up the stove pipe, left us all with our own nervous thoughts.

My mother kept the fire in the wood stove going as long as she could to keep us warm in the kitchen. The rest of the house grew colder by the minute. I knew that once the fire in the stove went out, there would be no heat until morning. I went to bed early, to get under the safety of the covers and the coats that were layered on top. I pulled the pile closer, burying my face and drawing comfort from the weight of the stack on top of me.

Later, in pitch darkness, I awoke to the roar of the raging wind and felt the cold breeze brush in faint gusts across my face. I dug deeper under the covers, the sound of each gust tightening the knot in my stomach.

When I awoke again, it was to the sound of my father talking to Daryl. In his voice I heard the desperation of the cattle in the corral, their freezing bodies whipped by the lashing wind. I imagined them huddled together as they always did when it was cold, drawing warmth from each others' bodies.

Unable to sleep and not wanting to be by myself, I crept out from under the covers. I shivered as I looked at the clothes waiting for me on the chair beside my bed. Gingerly, I tested the linoleum with my toes. A jolt went through my body. I set both feet on the floor and in a frenzy, pulled on my pants and shirt. The warmth of the long johns I had slept in saved me.

My father and Daryl were outside. Even in the blizzard the cattle had to drink. But the pump was frozen. My father struggled through the drifts of snow with boiling water to melt the ice. By the time he got to the pump, the water was too cold.

They retreated into the house. They looked grim. Cattle were collapsing, dying.

They tried again, with frozen faces and tearing eyes, to dismantle the pump. Together they carried it, encased in ice and snow, into the house and laid it in front of the stove. Water drained from its lifeless mouth onto the kitchen floor.

They left the house, summoning every last ounce of energy to reconnect the pump. It worked. The cattle drank.

We survived.

Canada vs. Russia!

Nothing it seemed would be a greater contest. The game had been on everyone's lips for weeks, Canada against Russia! Now, Leizer and Joe were in the car, glued to the radio. They didn't invite me to join them, so I hung out on the driveway, straining to hear through the open windows. I didn't know where they were playing but the announcer's voice was tinny so I guessed that it was far away.

As soon as the game got started, I saw Joe biting his nails, tightening his fist and clenching his teeth each time the Russians came close to scoring.

"He shoots! He scores!" The crowd went wild. I couldn't make out what the announcer was saying but I knew that the Canadians had put one away. I moved closer. I glanced inside to see my brothers' reactions. I heard Joe say, "They'll come back. They have time." I couldn't tell what Leizer was thinking.

They battled on, the announcer sounding like he could barely keep up with the action. The Canadians took a penalty. A chance for the Russians but they didn't score. Back to even strength and then, seconds later, "He scores!" Joe shouted, "Aha! I told you it's not over!"

At the window, I said, "I think I know who you want to win." They both looked at me blankly but didn't reply. It's all I dared to say but I was sure that it was the Russians. Why? Why the Russians? Could it be because of the War? They had said that the Russian army liberated them from certain death in the concentration camp. But that was so long ago. It wasn't fair.

The game went on, but without me. I didn't know how to feel so I walked away, across the yard. I found myself with Boobie and patted his head. He licked my face, looking up, his eyes pleading for me to play with him.

In the distance I heard the faint sound of the radio, the crowd erupting. This time it went on forever.

The game was over. We had won.

But there was no one to cheer with.

Endless

School was over for the summer. I was on holidays at last and this time it was special. I was visiting Leizer and Maggi, in Winnipeg. They thought it would be a good idea for me to spend some time in the big city.

It was night. We were all asleep. The phone rang. Leizer answered. Muffled sounds in the bedroom. Who could it be?

Maggi was up, going into the kitchen next to the living room where I slept on the couch. She didn't say anything but was busy making coffee. "I'll pick you up in twenty minutes," I heard Leizer say, before he hung up the phone. He came into the living room. I was sitting up, the blankets covering my legs. I was feeling suddenly very anxious.

Leizer came up to me and said, "Dad has been in an accident. He's in the hospital. We're going to Regina."

I didn't ask anything. I tried to get dressed but my hands were shaking and I was cold. I was scared. I had to go to the bathroom.

I got into the car with Maggi and Leizer. Nobody was talking. We drove to the Geidigers' house. Sonia was waiting on the driveway in the dark, with Hershel. She got into the back seat with me. Leizer got out and talked to Hershel. So much whispering. He got back in and we drove off.

Leizer didn't say a word. We made it onto the highway where he sped up. Ninety miles an hour. I had never travelled so fast in my life. I thought about my dad but didn't know what to think.

We got to Regina in just a few hours. We met my mother, Joe and his wife, Suzie, in a house that belonged to a family I didn't know.

My mother and I found ourselves in the back yard. She looked shrunken. "It's not good, Sammy," she said. I told her that everything would be OK. I didn't know what else to say. I didn't know what else to think.

My mother, Leizer, Joe and Sonia drove to the hospital. They left me alone in the house. They told me that there was no need for me to go.

I stayed. There was nobody to talk to. I reasoned that since they went without me, my father must be better. They just didn't want me to get upset.

Hours went by. They pulled into the driveway. Something wasn't right. My mother was crying uncontrollably. Sonia was holding her.

My father was dead.

I ran into the bathroom and locked the door. More than anything, I wanted to cry. But I couldn't. I didn't want anyone to see me.

Somebody wanted to come into the bathroom. I didn't let them in. I stayed there, locked away. I came out a long time later. Nobody said anything to me.

***

My father's funeral was at the synagogue in Regina. All the adults from the colony were there and some of the big boys too. My mother, Leizer, Joe and I gathered around my father's casket. I reached out to touch it, to say my last good-bye. I couldn't believe that this was happening. That I would never see my dad again. That this wooden box was all that was left. Just before leaving on my trip to Winnipeg, I had promised him that I would pray every morning. Now he would never know.

After the service we drove to the cemetery. My mother was crying, Sonia barely able to restrain her. I watched in horrid disbelief as they lowered my father into the ground. We came back to the house.

Everyone was ashen, silent. Then we prepared to leave, to return to the farm. I moved along with the others. Into the car, onto the highway.

People gathered at our house. Everyone I could think of. Someone called for quiet and began the memorial service. My mother and brothers recited the Kaddish, the prayer for the dead. My father hadn't taught me the prayer, so I stared mutely into my siddur.

People keep coming every day. There was more talking now. As I wove in and out among the men, I heard them say...

"How did it happen? How did the tractor end up in the ditch?"

"He fell off and hit his head on a rock. That's where Joe found him."

"The ambulance took him to Weyburn but Dr. Decter said he couldn't do anything and sent him to Regina."

***

It was mid-afternoon. The people who came to pray had not arrived yet. Leizer said that he was going to where the accident happened and asked whether I wanted to come along. I wanted that very much, but it scared me. We drove along Highway 18 toward the road that led to the slough where Joe and my father were going to be haying. After a while, Leizer slowed the car and we turned off the highway.

The dirt road started out flat and then dipped sharply, a dizzying descent to the slough, far below. Just as my father would have seen it.

Seconds later we saw the tractor on our left, its front end up against the far side of the ditch. Leizer stopped the car and we got out. Right in front of us I saw, in the dirt, the gouges of the two front tractor tires cutting sharply to the left across the road. My eyes took me to a huge boulder that rested silently in the middle of the ditch, beside the tractor.

I glared at everything. Angry at the rock that took my father's life. Angry at the road, so high, so steep. Angry that he didn't know how to drive. I didn't say anything. I felt a gnawing ache in my stomach. An endless pain.

***

There was a letter from my uncle Zelig, in Israel. My father's brother. My mother read it to herself. She wiped the tears away with her hands. I didn't want her to read it to me. I didn't want to get upset. But another part of me wanted to know what it said.

She read from the letter, "He survived the concentration camp just to have to die on a rock in a faraway field."

He did almost die in the concentration camp. My brothers were young then, like me, and they almost lost him there.

I did lose him, here.

A Nightmare

They were carving a dirt road into the field on the other side of the gravel highway that ran past our farm. I watched them from our yard and wondered at the mess of trucks and tractors moving large metal shapes that made even less sense than my own scattered toys.

Days later, as if by magic, tall circular tanks stood shiny and bright beside an oil well pump, mindlessly, repeatedly nodding its head. At the top of a towering pipe, a yellow and orange flame billowed in the wind. From the peak of the flame, black smoke twisted into the clear blue sky.

The trucks and crews were gone. There was only silence. Once in a long while a tanker truck paid the pump a visit.

From time to time, my mother talked about the oil well. About the constant flame that escaped from that tall, tall pipe. She said that someone might throw us into that flame.

I said nothing, too afraid to ask for more.

Who, I wondered, would do such a thing? Why was she even thinking such thoughts?

I saw in her face that she believed it really could happen.

I saw that it had happened before.

On Guard

The air was severe, the cold mirrored in the silvery moon and frost of countless stars.

Inside, my mother and I were warmed by heat blasting from the furnace vents.

It was late. My eyes were tired, dimming with the flickering flame of the coal oil lamp on the kitchen table, where I did my homework. Where I remembered my father reading and re-reading his Yiddish newspapers. Where he had rolled cigarette stubs into cigarettes.

I heard the steady rumble of the furnace down below, saving my mother and me from the deadly cold. The furnace that Leizer had bought. The monster whose sounds I did not trust.

I pulled the rope and raised the trap door in the middle of our kitchen floor. I climbed slowly, carefully, down the ladder to the cellar. The faint light descended with me and dissolved into the earthen pit. I turned on my flashlight and found my way between the furnace and the rough dirt walls. I reached the front of the furnace, sat on the ground and watched the flames burning in its iron belly.

Here, if something went wrong, I would know. In time for us to escape.

From time to time the embers collapsed in a rush of sparks, making way for more coal that burned slowly into the night, lulling me to sleep.

I was awakened by my mother's voice, "you have school tomorrow." As always, she didn't pressure me to come upstairs. Glad perhaps that I was standing guard.

Much later, I climbed the ladder. Went to my bed. More tired than certain that we were safe.

Pennies

We're leaving today – the farm and everything else. We're moving to Winnipeg. To live with Leizer and Maggi until we find a place of our own. Joe will be coming back here to his home in Oungre, to Suzie. For my mother and me everything is going to change.

I see sadness on my mother's face as she stuffs things into boxes and bags to be put in the truck. Joe is loading them one by one. We'll be off soon.

I walk around the yard one last time, restless. Boobie is on his chain lying on the ground watching me, his head nestled between his paws, only his eyes darting here and there. I don't go over to him. I can't say good-bye.

I want to leave something behind. Something I might come back to one day. The only thing I have is my glass jar of pennies. I get it from the house. I find a spot under our kitchen window and dig a hole with a small hand shovel from the tool shed. I hurry so that no one will see me. I lay the jar gently on its side and cover the hole with dirt and finally with gravel so no one will be able to tell. I don't worry about finding it again because if I come back, I'll just dig and dig until I find it. It's my hidden treasure, a part of me that won't ever leave.

When we get into the truck, I sit in the middle, between Joe and my mother. Joe puts the truck into gear and we pull away slowly, up the driveway toward the gravel road. The truck sways over the familiar dips and bumps. With a final nudge of the gas pedal, Joe pushes the truck onto the road, the one that takes us to Weyburn, only this time we're not going there at all.

I don't look back but imagine the farm in the blazing morning sun, watching us leave. I imagine the buildings getting smaller and smaller. Boobie getting up to walk around his barrel, his chain hanging from his neck, lapping what's left of the milk my mother left him. Suddenly, I feel my eyes welling up with tears that I don't want anyone to see. I don't want to be made fun of, especially not now. My mother and Joe are silent, thinking their own thoughts. Maybe they miss my dad too.

Words

An Occasional Thought

What you did today will get you there tomorrow.

Thank you, Elvis, for liberating the lower half of North America.

Science enables us to live; art makes life worth living.

If it weren't for children, how would we ever learn?

It takes doing.

"I'm alive and living" or, "I'm alive and dying."

The world has already been created – what more do you want to do?

Don't ask, "What do you want to be?" Ask, "What do you want to become?"

To get something done, someone has to own it.

Don't rush to get the unwanted answer.

Literature is ultimately about the liberation of the human spirit.

It's not enough to remember your history, you have to live it.

Spirituality is less about finding the profound experience than it is about experiencing the profound.

One choice is as bad as the other, except that one is worse.

Don't let tomorrow ruin today.

Advancing is good if you're going in the right direction.

If you're happy, it's easy to be.

Moments

Here is the CBC News...

Listening to the radio was for us no casual matter. My parents and older brothers were survivors of the Holocaust, newly arrived in the early 1950s to a Jewish farming colony in southern Saskatchewan. Despite the challenges of a strange, new language, the radio, and more particularly the CBC, provided them with a window to our new homeland and an occasional link to the world they had left behind. For me, a young boy of about ten, it was the gateway to a kaleidoscope of life and events I could hardly imagine. Here are three childhood memories of newscasts of that time that shaped the world.

The Rosenbergs
(1953)

Every hour life comes to a halt. We listen to the news, our eyes fixed on the radio.

"What are they saying?" my mother asks. My father, anguished, waits for an answer.

"Nothing. It's all up to the President," my brother Joe replies, the strain evident in his voice.

More bulletins. Julius and Ethel Rosenberg are being prepared for execution. Husband and wife. Found guilty of giving the Russians secrets to the bomb.

"Is it possible? Why kill them even if they did these things," I wonder but don't dare to ask.

"They have to blame somebody, so they're blaming the Jews. Nothing has changed," my father declares.

Joe's last hope is written on his face. "It can't happen in America," he says.

It's erev Shabbos.

The radio crackles. There will be no pardon. Not even a delay.

Hours later, the announcer reports that they are dead.

Death enters our house. Disbelief. Fear. Silence.

Outside, I catch the sun nearing the horizon.

Miles above, a vapour trail led by a silver speck traces across the sky. Another military plane protecting us from the Russians.

They say that we are safer now.

The Rosenbergs are dead.

Sinai War
(1956)

The threat of war is heavy in the air.

Shooting across the border. Israeli soldiers, the victims of snipers.

I recognize his voice on the radio. Nasser, the President of Egypt, threatening Israel's destruction.

Fear is in my parents' voices. Another war. Lives in danger once again. Our family is there.

I sense my brothers' frustration. Too far to join the coming fight.

What will happen? To Israel? To us?

In the morning we hear the news. War. Millions aligned against us.

Reports of death. Tanks and planes. Speeches. A tidal wave of hate.

"Bring us your atlas," my brothers ask. The one I just got.

With a pencil they carve black arrows across the Sinai.

I stare at the scars.

My atlas.

A casualty of war.

Sputnik
(1957)

"Here is the six o'clock news. History was made today when the Soviet Union launched the first satellite ever to orbit the earth. The satellite entered an orbit at..." My brother Joe and I are in the living room. He looks serious, staring at the radio, but says nothing.

My mother asks him to shut it off. It's almost Shabbos.

She blesses the candles and asks us to come to the table. My father rises to recite the Kiddush. He drinks from the cup of wine and blesses the challah. We savour my mother's Shabbos meal.

"I heard them talking a whole day on the radio about the satellite," my mother says, knowing that the subject is still on Joe's mind, "but I don't really understand. What exactly did they do?"

Joe explains, "The Russians shot a rocket far up into the sky and instead of falling back down, it's going to stay up, go around the earth and send radio signals back."

"And what about the Americans?" she asks.

"That's the point. They haven't done it yet. The Russians are first and who knows if the Americans will ever catch up? No one knows where this will end. They might even get to the moon."

"It's all made up," my father says, breaking his silence. "They aren't going around the earth. They're not going anywhere. Not to the moon. Nowhere."

"Dad," Joe replies, "they will go to the moon. It's only a matter of time."

"Nowhere! They tried it with the Tower of Babel and we know how that ended. If God had wanted us to be on the moon he would have put us there. It's all propaganda – the Russians and the Americans are trying to outdo each other and all the fools are believing it."

I look from one to the other and at the clock. Time for the news, an update on what's happening. Could it all be fake? I wonder. Are the Russians just scaring us?

I glance at the radio. It's off. It's Shabbos.

How Did This Dog Happen?

It snuck up gradually, like the creeping realization of some fundamental truth that won't be denied and then it burst upon us. It happened in the morning when I take Ronnie to the subway, the start of her daily trip to work. When we chat about random things or try to squeeze in an important piece of business that we forgot to deal with the night before.

"I hate this darkness," I grumble as we weave around the snow banks. "Months of it and it's going to get worse." Ronnie doesn't bother to answer. I know she agrees.

"I think we need a dog," Ronnie says, almost to herself. But I hear her and it registers. I wonder at how evenly I take it. Almost as if I could have said it myself. And instantly, I just know that our lives have changed. Forever.

I don't ask her why. I can feel it in my bones – an idea whose time has come. Could it be because she thinks I'm getting bored at home, in my retirement? Or that our kids, though in their twenties, could use a buddy? Or, could it be the constant refrain of friends talking about their grandchildren?

"It would be good for the kids." I offer, just as a red light begins to flash in the corner of my brain.

"But who is going to take care of it?" I ask, my heart suddenly searching for an exit from my chest. "I sure don't want to be the one going out in the snow and sleet to walk the dog at five in the morning all winter."

Ronnie knows me too well. That evening we go on line, make some phone calls and, three peaceful months later, we pick up a brand new Havanese puppy whose name was destined by the stars to be – Rusty.

It's now three weeks later. My kids have regressed to something in the order of five or six and Ronnie has rediscovered a voice I haven't heard since Evan and Elana were babies. What is clearly one of the simplest names in the English language has become an entire high-pitched sentence: Russ...Teeee?!"

The sound is riveting. My ears perk up at the same time as Rusty's. Is something wrong? Whatever it is, I let Rusty go first. And it works. When I show up, Ronnie says, as if she's half-forgotten that I live here, "Oh, there you are. I was going to tell you something, but I've forgotten what..."

The notion that I'm entirely dispensable has become contagious. They all arrive sooner or later – Ronnie and Elana from work, and Evan, who has discovered that there is day after night, from his room. All I'm now good for is to answer the only question they seem capable of asking, "Where's Rusty?"

They've all left now. Rusty and I are alone. I've fed him and like a hovering hawk I'm watching, watching until, with equal portions of amazement and disbelief, I see it: the telltale twist of his body, the eyes searching for a private spot. As if my life depends on it, I make a dash for him, scoop him up in one hand while struggling to maneuver my arm into a coat sleeve with the other. My hat is gripped firmly between my teeth and I'm praying that my gloves are in my pocket. Oh, and I need a bag! Desperately, I drop my hat and prepare to pick the plastic bag up with my teeth. I stare at it. I know it's empty but I just can't do it. Rusty is squirming, trying to break free. Frantically, I slide the glass doors open and am about to step outside. I'm in my socks!

Just then the phone rings. Instinctively, I push the speaker button, immediately regretting what I've done.

"How's Rusty?" Ronnie asks buoyantly.

"Fine!" I shout, while in a sweeping motion that would rival the best of Baryshnikov, I offer Rusty to the snow-covered steps. "I'm just putting him outside to do his business and I'll call you right back."

"Oh, OK!" she replies, the glee in her voice palpable. "Let me know what happens!"

In the evening, not long after dinner, my eyelids droop and my body draws me to the couch for a nap. I couldn't be happier. Rusty, asleep on Ronnie's lap, opens one eye to see where I am going, the ringer on the phone is off and the lights on the front porch are out. Only an earthquake can get me now.

On the edge of sleep, I feel that deep contentment that tells me I'm as near to semiconsciousness as you can get. Numbing nirvana... and,... and, an unmistakable sensation that something is snuggling up against me, burrowing its way relentlessly toward my head. I resist the thought, willing it away into my dreams. Not a chance. It's getting closer and then, with an explosive burst of energy it erupts, a fierce nose in my face and a slobbering lick across my mouth.

My hand shoots up and my eyes squeeze shut in a vain attempt at self-defence. Somewhere in the dark recesses of my mind, in the hazy remnants of my shattered sleep, a question begins to form: how did this happen? I can't fathom an answer. I don't remember a thing. Until, a moment later, when I hear that inimitable, loving call:

"Russ...Teeee?!"

Images

Day One

The ringing of the telephone startled her. Only Boris knew Sara's number.

"Is everything in order?" asked the familiar voice on the other end.

"Yes."

"I've reserved seats 5 and 6 in Row G at the opera." He hung up. Anything more could betray them to whoever might be listening. Sara ached to talk to him but this was not the time.

In her copy of Thomas Hardy's *The Return of the Native* she turned to page 7, corresponding to the place of the letter G in the alphabet, and found line 5. She memorized the words. She would look for them and the coded message in today's issue of *Le Monde*, in the personal section.

She closed the website and her laptop, then put on her coat. It had rained in the morning and it was still threatening.

"Come, Gigi," she called. She had been assigned the dog by Boris, in charge of their Paris mission. He had told her that the three-year-old Havanese was trained and came from the kennel of a Mossad operative, its clinging nature ideal for Sara's needs. Gigi was a necessary cover, he had explained, but under no circumstances was she to endanger herself or the operation to save the dog if things went wrong. Gigi had been dropped off at her apartment by a young man she had never met and who did not introduce himself. Alone with the dog, she had proceeded cautiously, more than a little skeptical of how this would turn out. She was not a dog lover and had never owned a pet.

They walked down the hall toward the elevators, Sara listening for any sounds that might reveal a watchful eye. She stepped onto the cobbled street, continuing in the direction of the intersection where the newspaper stand was always a hub of activity. As she rounded the corner, she deliberately stopped at the baker's stall and asked for a croissant. She continued on, bought a newspaper and casually flipped through the sections, pretending to check the headlines.

"Let's go home, Gigi," she said, stuffing the folded newspaper into her bag. She hesitated, noticing the pleading look in Gigi's eyes and broke off a tiny piece of the croissant. Gigi swallowed it whole and looked up at Sara, hoping for more.

Ahmed noticed the woman from his seat at a small table in front of the cafe across the street. He sensed an alertness in the woman's manner. He kept his eyes on her as she bought her pastry and proceeded to pick up a newspaper. Although the presence of the dog made him somewhat uncertain, there was a stiffness about the way she treated it that added to his suspicion. Could she be part of the Mossad team that they expected would retaliate against the recent bombing of the Jewish community centre? His superiors had long believed that the Israelis kept a safe house in the area. He had been posted here to observe, his instructions clear: locate and report, do not engage.

With a nod to Farid at the cash register, he moved cautiously in the direction of the woman before she slipped away.

Sara felt eyes on her. She wasn't sure from where but it was the instinct that had saved her before. She wouldn't look around, forcing herself to stay focussed on behaving normally, though every nerve was on edge. She walked to the corner, retracing her footsteps. When she was out of view of the intersection, she turned again and quickly entered a smaller laneway. It would have to do, even if it was a dead-end. She gathered Gigi in her arms, praying that she would not betray them, and slid behind the metal dumpster parked along the wall. She reached for her pistol.

She heard the footsteps stop in the laneway where she had turned in. Only feet away from the dumpster. Someone was coming for her. She had nowhere to go. The silence told Ahmed that she was there, behind the dumpster. Probably armed but likely protecting her dog. It would give him an edge. He recalled his orders, "Do not engage," and hesitated. If he walked on and let her go, he could follow her later. But she would lead him in meaningless directions. He might even lose her. She was trapped. If he captured her, she would make a great prize. He drew his automatic. He had to move in, now.

Sara heard the stealthy approaching footsteps. She threw the croissant to her left. Gigi instantly leapt after the food as Sara dove around the other side of the dumpster, crouching and firing at the target. Ahmed stared at the dog in disbelief as he absorbed each bullet. He sank to the ground, his pistol dropping from his hand.

She knew that the man might not be alone. There was no time to retrieve documents from his body. She walked quickly to the end of the laneway, checking to see whether anyone was coming. Not yet, she calculated, although the sound of the shots would have alerted any accomplice the man had. In as nonchalant a manner as she could manage, Sara walked on, Gigi keeping pace at her side. She turned at the first corner, drawing any followers away from the direction to her apartment. She would have to contact Boris to alert him to what had happened and get further instructions. If her cover was blown, her entire mission might change. Her stomach tightened at the thought that she hadn't even read the coded message in *Le Monde*.

The dog had been a good cover, she thought, but if someone had seen them, they would be more visible now. She picked Gigi up and quickened her pace. The dog's head grazed her cheek. She glanced down and it instinctively looked up at her.

"I owe you one, Gigi," she heard herself say, astonished at her own words.

Homeless

His eyes still closed, Rick drifted with the rhythm of the traffic, the occasional truck drowning out the steady hum of cars. It was the sirens that sent a shiver up his spine and roused him from his dreams.

He climbed out from under the covers of the sagging cot onto the splintered wooden floor. The barren walls, the yellow fixture caked with the dust of ages, the rust-stained sink, were all disheartening. It was a dismal room but it reminded him that he was out of jail, far from the sanitized surroundings where clean and shiny had not kept him from despair. He recalled an earlier life. The images were right there with him, just as they had been in prison: the love of his parents, the upscale neighbourhood where he had grown up, the painful realization that so much in life was measured by what a person had accomplished, his friends going on to university with a certainty that he envied, his own life a darkened void, plagued by indecision. He was a failure. He escaped.

Between odd jobs he took to roaming the city. He found himself on an afternoon at a small park a stone's throw away from the heart of the business district. An older man in shabby clothes sat at the end of a worn green bench, his gaze fixed on the trodden grass. Rick settled on the bench, at first saying nothing, then chancing an introduction.

"Hi, my name is Rick."

The man did not reply.

A moment later, Rick tried again. "I've never hung out here before. It's very peaceful."

The man grunted.

Rick began to get up when he heard, barely above a whisper, "I'm Don."

He sat down and waited, unsure of what to say.

"I've been living here for two years. Ever since my wife died."

"Oh, I'm sorry," Rick said, glancing at the man hunched over in his crumpled jacket, worn jeans and broken shoes. Overgrown stubble covered his face. His hair stuck out from under his cap, tangled and greasy.

"I used to work over there," Don said without looking up.

Rick cast his eyes about to the gleaming office towers. He couldn't imagine...

"Yes there, where you're looking," he continued. "I was an advisor in an investment firm. On the forty-third floor. I was one of the best."

Rick was about to ask what happened, when Don went on.

"After she died, it all ended. Nobody understands." He fell silent.

From time to time Rick joined Don on the bench and tried to talk to him. Don said nothing, as if their conversation had never happened.

Rick felt a solitude here that he hadn't found anywhere else. His mind didn't crash into walls. It coasted, gently. Without money, he drifted into begging for coins like the others in the park. He managed to collect just enough to keep going. Then he made his first mistake. As he reached for the wallet through the car window, someone grabbed him from behind. He struggled to get free, striking back fiercely with his elbow. It found its mark. He heard a crack. He didn't run.

Amidst these thoughts, he took stock of his face in the stained bathroom mirror and washed up, relishing every newborn sensation. He decided not to make any plans today, to give himself a chance simply to be. But hard as he tried, he couldn't escape the familiar thoughts gnawing at the edges. He had to find a job, to repay his friend Dennis for arranging this room. And he had to stay out of trouble. He hoped that his parole officer would be a decent person.

Rick stepped into a nearby coffee shop, filling his lungs with the stirring aroma that met him at the door. The place was crowded with people, some alone, others chatting with a friend or colleague. He was glad to find a perch at the window. He looked out onto the street where a crew was working on a problem underground. As the workers went into and out of the manhole, he wondered about all the systems that supported life in the city. It might be an interesting subject to explore some day.

It was a while since he'd been on a streetcar, preferring to walk when he could. He relaxed with the rhythmic clatter of the wheels and studied the people on the sidewalk. Their pace seemed to quicken with every intersection as they neared the hub of the city. He felt eyes on him too. Was it written on his face? Could they tell that he'd just gotten out? He adjusted himself in his seat, taking up a little more room than he needed, discouraging anyone from sitting beside him.

Rick thought of calling Dennis but decided to do it later. For now, he needed some space. He got off the streetcar and walked toward the old city hall and the department store windows that never failed to stir his imagination. He passed by the park where he'd last seen Don and wondered what became of him. He recalled the familiar feelings. Here no one asked questions. It was up to you whether you talked or just listened. Life was simple and beautiful in its own way. But he was choosing a better path.

Rick approached the massive displays, his eyes settling on an arrangement of camping gear. The scene reminded him of the trip he'd taken with his parents to the Maritimes, when he finished high school. He would never forget the awesome sight of the whales off the coast of Newfoundland. None of his pictures captured the beauty and grace of these giants.

He was about to move on when he saw their reflection in the glass. Two policemen coming up behind him. He turned to face them, his jaws tight, every muscle tense.

"Rick, is that you?" asked one of the officers. "It's me, Jensen," he continued. "You're out? Has it been three months already?"

"It's me," Rick replied to the man he'd recognized immediately as his arresting officer.

"So, just hanging out?"

"Just taking in the sights," Rick said, conscious of the other officer watching him.

"Well, keep it that way. Don't break my heart." Jensen and his partner exchanged looks and moved on as quickly as they had arrived.

Rick swallowed. Jensen's words echoed in his mind as he watched the officers get into their car and drive away. "Don't break my heart." It was more than a warning. Jensen expected him to break the law. A wave of doubt swept over him. Was Jensen right? Would he succeed? There were so many obstacles to overcome.

He set out slowly, in no particular direction, a growing emptiness inside. He saw only the sidewalk before his feet, one step and another. He found himself at the edge of the park. He saw the spot where he'd begged for coins, the tree under which he'd slept. He recognized many of the men too, some standing alone, their bundles tucked beside them, others in pairs, sharing a smoke. He looked at the cars parked along the street, where it had all happened.

He continued into the park, to the familiar bench where Don had opened his heart. He rested there, watching the hopeful pigeons at his feet. He thought of Dennis. He would call him tomorrow. He lay down, tightening his jacket around his chest. It would be sundown soon.

Gentle Paces

He navigated absent-mindedly through the crowd at his customary Starbucks, across from City Hall. Although he recognized many of the faces, he was grateful that no one knew him. It allowed him to prolong his waking slumber for a few minutes more before he had to admit that the day had actually begun. Through his mental haze he noticed the woman at the condiments stand reaching for her cup, momentarily distracted by something she saw outside the window. He watched motionless as the back of her hand struck the side of the cup, knocking it over. He sprang into action trying to save the drink but failed and apologized. Their eyes met.

"I'll get you another cup," he offered.

"Please no, don't bother. It was my fault. I'm already late for work."

"No," he replied, "please wait here."

He made his way to the counter and ordered two coffees. Moments later, he returned. She was still standing where he'd left her.

"I got myself one too," he said, smiling, "so don't feel bad. Would you like to sit down? I also bought us a couple of chairs."

She laughed, thinking, why not, as they both revisited the condiments stand. He had been kind enough, more in tempering her embarrassment than in getting her coffee, though that too was a generous gesture. He had a reserved casualness that set her at ease, but his appearance left her somewhat uncertain. She noted that he wore a pale green T-shirt with no markings and weathered but clean blue jeans. His shoes, however, told a different story. Originally white, his runners were thick with the grime of the street.

He saw her glance at his shoes but said nothing. She was a picture of perfection, her long brown hair falling straight beside her bright, oval face, its tanned complexion made more dramatic still by her sparkling brown eyes. He could see without staring that unlike him, she wore brilliant white tennis shoes and socks. They fit perfectly with the rest of her appearance.

"I like this place," he declared as they took their seats, "I've been coming here for years." She didn't reply but he instantly sensed that she must be wondering the obvious. "Oh, it's not a hangout, it's where I come to think about my writing. It's a great place for that."

"Oh, you're a writer," she remarked.

He smiled, affirming what he'd said, enjoying the obvious relief in her voice.

"One of those, yes."

"Sorry, I didn't mean..."

"No, it's OK," he interrupted. "With shoes like these, who knows?"

They both laughed heartily.

Still enjoying the moment he said, "I'm Dennis."

"I'm Jackie," she replied. They held each other's gaze for just a moment, both keenly aware that they were strangers.

"And where do your shoes take you, Jackie?" he asked, exaggerating a raised eyebrow.

"Oh, nothing as interesting as writing, but I do read a bit. Mostly political reviews to keep our clients informed of news that is relevant to their enterprise. It's hard for executives to keep up and get a picture of what's going on these days. We try to do it for them."

"Fascinating. But it sounds like you're not giving yourself enough credit. Your writing must be superb to be able to consolidate the masses of information into a meaningful text."

She smiled at his observation. It was true. Their agency lived and died by the quality of the team's analysis.

He caught her just then, glancing at her watch. "I should get going," he said, pretending he hadn't seen anything.

"Yes, I have to go too," she replied as they both got up to leave.

"My office is just around the corner," she said, as they left the coffee shop.

"I'll walk you to the light," he offered, "and then I'm plunging into the masses down there."

He pointed in the direction of the intersection congested with pedestrians.

"I enjoyed the chat," he continued. "I hope we can spill some coffee again some time."

"I don't come here every day," she said. "But," she added, "Friday morning coffees are a must. It helps me get the weekend going early."

"See you then," he smiled and waved as she rounded the corner.

A Boundless Journey

This was Pierre's first trip with his parents to Honfleur, where his father had often come with his family when he was a boy. Pierre's grandparents had died before he was born but his father kept their memory and his own enchantment with Honfleur alive in the bedtime stories that he told his son.

Today, as he and his parents walked among the ancient buildings that he had heard so much about, Pierre could almost hear the clip clop sounds of horses pulling wagons in the cobbled streets. He imagined crowds of people just as now, eagerly making their way to the banks of the river that coursed through the town.

Pierre held his mother's hand as they strolled along. Then, rounding a corner, they came upon a breathtaking view of the river, glistening white sailboats moored at its sides. The adjoining sidewalks were bounded by tall, narrow buildings, spots of painted curtains visible in their windows and brilliant awnings sheltering the crowded streets.

He was the first to see it, commanding a grassy knoll at the end of the walkway. He pulled his hand free and ran toward it but stopped suddenly, dazzled by the beauty of the carousel. He had never seen such a wonder. The outside of the massive crown was adorned with mirrored shields that spoke of mysteries and haunted dreams. The shields were separated by gigantic diamonds that must have been stolen by murderous pirates from the treasure chests of kings. A gold ceiling adorned the enormous wheel. In it were embedded paintings of swordsmen in the throes of battle with daunting foes; others portrayed warriors bounding off on horseback, the conquest of a maiden in their arms, their victory celebrated by a sea of lights.

Beneath these images he saw scores of horses thundering toward him. He leapt onto the fiercest stallion, narrowly avoiding a deadly spill into a gaping chasm. He charged fearlessly across the void, galloping into the wind, pursued by legions of loyal soldiers.

Sketches

The Reluctant Shopper

Translated from the all-Yiddish CD, S'helft Nisht Keyn Krekhtsn! (There's No Use Complaining!) *Note: Any resemblance in this story to real names and places is purely coincidental.*

I don't know whether it's just us or in every family that everyone pokes his nose into everybody else's business.

Each Sunday, the whole gang, my brothers, their wives and their kids get together at our house. And, since my own kids and my nieces and nephews are all grown up, we're blessed not only with the mouth-watering foods that my wife so lovingly prepares but also with bountiful discussions about the latest political issues, all sorts of philosophical questions and always, our day-to-day troubles.

And so, everything was going swimmingly last week until I happened to mention, with a sigh befitting my age, that I needed to buy myself a new pair of pants.

All at once, ten voices erupted. Each with an opinion about where I should buy the pants, who I should buy them from and what sort of fabric and style I should choose. Instantly, the room became a bazaar. And nobody cared a fig about what I thought.

After a few minutes they settled down and decided that whatever pants I bought, I had to get them at the Galaxy Shopping Centre, from Schwartz's Fine Fabrics. And with that they left me alone.

As for me, I realized that if I wanted to avoid a battle the next time around, I'd simply have to go along.

And so, the day arrives and I set off for the Galaxy. A half-hour later, I see the sparkling rooftops of the massive stores in the distance. Wonderful. But as I get closer, I get the feeling that the entire city has converged here today to snap up the bargains. I drive around endlessly, looking for a parking spot, and just when I find one, I see that there are already other cars waiting and that out of each window hangs an embittered face with crazed eyes threatening that if I even dream of taking the next parking spot, I should be prepared to die.

With God's help I find a spot. I crawl out of my car and begin to drag myself to the entrance to the shopping centre. Finally I get there, look around and find a sea of stores. But no sign of Schwartz's.

There are hordes of people everywhere. They're trooping and lugging. Everyone loaded down with bags of stuff. I'm going nowhere. I'm frozen. Lost. But, all at once I notice a map on top of a large table surrounded by people. I inch closer and see that they are all bent over the table, with tortured looks on their faces. Whether they are actually searching for something or just trying to find the quickest way out of here is anybody's guess.

I squeeze through to the map and discover that Schwartz's is a mere five aisles to the left and three aisles up from where I am.

I'm schlepping yet again, until at last I get to my store. I barely enter, when I'm approached by a greeter. He confronts me with such a hearty "Welcome!" that you would think that I had single-handedly saved his life. I smile and no sooner do I return his greeting, than he forgets about me completely and rushes off to another customer.

I look around and see that I'm surrounded by an entire landscape of tables full of merchandise. Customers are gathered at the tables, checking out the goods. But there isn't a single salesperson in sight. So I ask one of the customers whether he knows where I might find a pair of pants. He gives me a look and tells me that if I follow the signs dangling from the ceiling, I'll find my way to the pants.

So now I'm searching the heavens and trudging once again.

According to the signs, there are all sorts of clothes here, but for the life of me I don't see any pants. So I keep going until I do find – not pants, but shirts. Countless shirts. All styles, colours and sizes stretch as far as the eye can see. But no pants.

So once again I'm searching for a salesman. Forget it. But I notice a cash register on a table in the distance. I make my way there, figuring that just maybe a salesman will crawl out from under the table and help me. No such luck. But I see that there is a phone beside the cash register and a sign beside the phone. The sign says that if a customer has a problem, he should simply pick up the phone and someone will answer and help.

I pick up the phone and am greeted by a cheerful voice. I explain that I'm standing among the shirts but that I can't find any pants. The voice asks me why I'm standing among the shirts if what I want is pants. I reply that I don't actually need shirts but that I simply can't find the pants. So he says that since I'm among the shirts, it would be a shame if I didn't buy myself a shirt and then went hunting for pants.

I ask why it's so important to him that I should buy a shirt. He explains that he works for the shirt department and that it's his job to sell shirts, not pants. Pants, he says, are another operator's business. And how, I ask him, do I find the operator for the pants? He answers that I'll first have to find the pants and among the pants I'll find a phone and with that phone I'll be able to get in touch with the right operator. By now my head is spinning. I say nothing and hang up.

I look around and think. Since I can't find any pants, maybe I really should buy myself a nice shirt and just get out of here. I settle on a few shirts in various styles and colours. I step into the change room, try the shirts on and pick two. But, since I don't know my way around these things, I can't tell whether the shirts suit me or not.

So I'm again looking for a salesman, this time just to get an opinion. But it's a waste of time because it looks like absolutely nobody works here. I have no choice but to go back to the phone at the cash register. I pick up the phone and the same cheery voice greets me.

I tell the voice that I've picked two shirts but that I don't know whether they suit me or not. Without hesitating he says that he's sure that they are both excellent choices and that I should buy them both. I reply that I'm not your ordinary customer and that I'm surprised that he would offer an opinion without even seeing the shirts. He says I'm right and that if I want to be sure of my shirts, I should first match them up with my pants. And he asks, "Have you managed to find your pants?"

My rage is overwhelming. "I HAVE NO PANTS!" I scream into the phone. "If I had pants I wouldn't need shirts! Don't mix me up! Make yourself crazy!"

I throw away the shirts and take off like a shot.

There are no salesmen! The phone is a waste of time! The greeter is running around like a chicken with his head cut off! There-is-no-one-to-talk-to!!!

My Computer

Translated from the all-Yiddish CD, S'helft Nisht Keyn Krekhtsn (There's No Use Complaining!)

I'd like to tell you what happened when my children recently talked me into buying a computer. I told them that I have enough problems with the contraptions that I already have. So why, I asked, do I need a computer?

They immediately explained that today you just can't live without a computer. And, since I want to live, I listened to my dear children and got myself a computer. You understand, of course, that buying a computer is not that simple. First of all, you have to know what to buy. And if you do know what to buy, you have to know where to buy. That's why I'm blessed to have, among all my nieces and nephews, one who is special, and he went with me to find a computer.

So we drive around until we arrive at a huge store where they say you can find the best and the biggest machines. Besides, they're supposed to be cheaper here than anywhere else. What can I say? It sounds good to me.

We go into the store and no sooner do the doors close behind us than we're hit with such a blast of music that my ears are splitting and I'm searching desperately for a place to escape. I glance at my nephew and see that he's standing there totally relaxed. Suddenly, it occurs to me, that maybe he's lost his hearing altogether and if so, this calamity is all my fault. But I take a closer look and see that he can hear. And I realize that the noise that shook me to my bones hasn't even touched him.

And as I stand there, beside my Moishele, I take a look around and see that the salesmen are making with the hands and the lips, talking to the shoppers, but I can't hear a thing. I take a few more steps and toward us comes one of these smiling salesmen. He too starts to flap his hands and his lips at Moishe. But, because Moishe is blessed, he can not only hear what the man is saying, he can understand him too. Before you know it they become fast friends and both look at me as I stand there, one helpless fool.

We finally finish and I'm ready to pay every penny they want from me. I'm happy, because to me it's worth parting with everything I own just to get out of here. At the cash, they promise me that I'll have to wait only a day or two for the computer to be delivered right to my home. I'm tempted to say that they should take their time, there's no rush. But it wouldn't be polite so I bite my tongue and pray silently for the computer to vanish so I can be spared another headache.

With God's help, the day arrives when they bring me a pile of boxes – my computer. And, because I'm not a complete fool, I asked a young man who knows about computers to come to my place and to shield me from disaster. Who knows what a computer can decide to do when it finds itself with a simple, innocent man like me?

It takes the young man only a minute to unpack the whole bundle. Boxes, books and wires are flying everywhere. And, before you know it, he tells me that everything is in order and that I can start playing on my computer. He explains a few things about the buttons and shows me how to run the machine.

I look at him as he talks, and smile and assure him that his every word is as clear as day. But inside, my heart is trembling, afraid that this fellow might leave without locking up the machine and that the computer might wake up during the night and cause a calamity. In the end the young man got me organized, and in the days that followed, I went to a special class to learn the proper way to handle a computer. I listened carefully to our teacher and understood clearly when he told us that we have nothing to be afraid of. That the computer won't explode. And it won't eat us up. And what's more, if something should go wrong, we have the warranty from the store and with that everything will be set right. With those few words he cursed me forever. Because suddenly I understood that my marriage to the computer is forever.

So I'm sitting there one afternoon at my computer. I press the large button and the computer immediately begins to rumble and belch. Good. I wait for all the noises and pictures to finish so I can start to look for something on the internet. If you don't know what the internet is, do me a favour and don't ask. I can only tell you that it brings to mind a huge noodle that stretches from one end of the world to the other and through that noodle, flow all kinds of communications.

A minute goes by and the computer is set.

Just then, my hand slips and I accidentally press a number of keys. I'm terrified. Not that I could have fallen and broken my neck. But at what problems I've caused by pressing the keys. I stare like a lost soul at the monitor and suddenly see printed in huge letters the words, "Illegal Procedure. Fatal Error." As I understand these words, I'm now in deep trouble. "Illegal" is bad enough. But my greatest fear comes from the words "fatal error." Fatal means dead, and so, it seems that I have unintentionally killed somebody.

I'm so perplexed that I barely remember what they told us in the class. That if we have a problem, whether by day or night, we should call a certain number and that they will help us. Finally I find the number and, sweating like someone going to the gallows, I dial the whole row of digits.

Someone picks up the phone and answers with a strange accent. I'm convinced that it's the police. In one minute, he asks me my name, my address and my phone number. And all these questions mean to me that before you know it someone will be at my door to arrest me. I gather up all my courage and ask the man, "Where are you?" He answers that he is in Calcutta. So I say to him that there isn't a place called Calcutta here in Toronto. He replies that Calcutta isn't in Toronto, it's in India.

Well, I think. At least he won't come running all the way from India just to arrest me. But sitting there in Calcutta, how can he help? He can't see me. He can hardly hear me. And with my total ignorance of computers he won't even be able to understand what I tell him.

But I have no choice. I say, tell me if it's possible accidentally to kill somebody with a computer. He is totally silent. So I think to myself that now that he knows what this is all about, he'll definitely send somebody to arrest me. I'm shaking all over again. But I ask him once more. I tell him this time that I slipped and accidentally pressed some keys on the computer and that the computer immediately told me that I had committed a fatal error. And what does that mean?

I'm sure that an hour goes by before he answers me. And still he doesn't answer. He starts to laugh uncontrollably. I'm afraid that he'll choke to death and won't answer me altogether. Finally, he settles down and manages to tell me that I haven't killed anyone. That this is just an expression in the world of computers. And he quickly gives me the remedy to fix my machine.

I hang up the phone and stare at the computer. I think to myself, why do I need this altogether. Who needs a computer? Who needs the internet? I don't want to communicate. And, if I do want noodles, I'll have soup.

The Bureaucrat

Translated and adapted from the all-Yiddish CD, S'helft Nisht Keyn Krekhtsn! (There's No Use Complaining!)

I've been slaving for thirty-three years. In an office. In a government office. Oh, you say, that's not work! What kind of work can that be if you sit there, in the lap of luxury, in a climate-controlled office all year, gazing out the window more than at your papers and so on.

Well, if life is so grand, why does every civil servant walk around looking so tortured? Why do we all look so depressed as though we are labouring under the strain of the entire world's troubles? I can see that you don't know. And that's the problem.

So I'll have to enlighten you as to what it means to work for the government.

My job is in the office of the Minister of Agriculture. But it hardly matters which minister. You understand that every minister is exceptional, consumed by the aim of creating a better world. Every minister is driven by one goal: that we should all achieve a better life, and that our children should live in a world of peace and joy. And, in order to achieve these lofty goals, they dedicate themselves entirely to their work, get paid hardly anything for their efforts and serve as models in decency to us all.

And this enormous burden that falls on the shoulders of the minister rests on my shoulders as a civil servant as well. Why? Well, you first have to understand that it doesn't even occur to a minister that his position might ever come to an end. He is convinced that God himself chose him for the job. But, just in case, he relies on me, his right hand, to ensure that all this is assured. And that's why all the bright ideas, all the important documents, every scheme and rumour have to cross my desk. So that I'll know what's going on in the ministry and be able to shield the minister from disaster.

And so, I arrive in my office one day and see from a distance that there is already a note waiting for me. I sit down and have a look. What does it say? It's a message from a director in our Ministry. He wants to see me immediately.

While I think about it, I pour myself a cup of coffee, go back to my seat and call the director. He answers, "Sholom Aleichem, this is Yankel Shpitzer."

"Good morning Yankel," I say. What would you like to talk to me about?

"We're publishing the projection of the size of this year's cherry crop. I think that the minister should be given the number ahead of time so that he can take proper credit for it."

"Slow down," I say. "Why don't we get together and talk this over."

In a blink of an eye he shows up in my doorway. He's so excited that he can hardly breathe.

I ask, "Yankel, what's the rush with the number? Explain it fully to me so that I can give the minister a proper briefing."

"The great news is that the size of this year's crop is the best we've ever had in the country's history," he proclaims. "And," he adds, "why is that important? Because with that big a crop we won't have to import any cherries this year. We won't have to worry about whether other countries will or won't sell them to us."

"I understand, Yankel, what you're saying, but if the number is that important, we have no choice but to be extra cautious." I sigh and say solemnly, "Yankel, you have truly performed an outstanding feat coming up with the projection. But you have to understand, Yankel, that we cannot reveal the number to the minister. The number must remain secret."

Yankel looks entirely perplexed. He asks, "What sense does that make? He has to know. Otherwise what's the point of all this work?"

"Well," I say, "please understand that the minister knows full well that we would sacrifice our lives for him. But what exactly we do, he doesn't know and at times, it's better that way."

Yankel stares at me as if I have just landed from another planet. Seeing the forlorn look on his face, I say, "Yankel, I see that you understand me very well and that we should never be too eager to solicit praise. Let's instead concern ourselves with saving the minister from a potential embarrassment."

Obviously upset, Yankel asks, "What kind of embarrassment? It's just the opposite. We have here an historic moment and you talk of embarrassment? What kind of nonsense is this?"

So I explain. "Here in our department, the minister is in his own domain. He's in no danger, everyone supports him, we all respect him, we believe everything he says, we run to carry out whatever he asks of us, and every word he utters is sacred. But as soon as he steps outside he has to contend with critics who want only to belittle him and to rob him of his position. And we, Yankel, are the ones who have to protect him."

Yankel stares at me incredulous.

So I go on. "Yankel, the minister can think that the yield of the crop is huge. He can even believe that it's greater than in all of recorded history. But he can't know it. He can "imagine" but he can't actually "know." Why? Because as long as it's only in his thoughts, he can come up with countless reasons for changing his mind. He can say on Monday that the crop will be bigger this year than last and Wednesday, he can say just the opposite, that the yield will be half of what it was before. Understand, Yankel, that whatever happens, the minister can't be the one to blame. And as long as he doesn't know anything, he's safe. That, Yankel, is why we can't give the number to the minister."

Yankel looks like he's going to pass out. He asks, "And what should I do if the minister sees me in the hallway and asks me himself what the size of the crop is going to be?"

I tell him, "Yankel, that's why you're a director, to know just what to do in such a situation. And you understand that sometimes if you try a little less, everyone is better off. In fact, after such a tremendous effort, you deserve to take a few days off until all this blows over. Take a rest and forget all about numbers and ministers and cherries."

I give him a friendly slap on the back and assure him that he has been a hero. And with that the conversation ends.

Before long, the minister wanders into my office. And what do you think? He's not a complete fool. He is convinced that the bureaucrats don't tell him the truth and want him to do only what they think is best, whether he agrees with it or not.

"What's new?" he asks.

"Well, Minister," I reply cautiously, "Yankel Shpitzer, the director of agricultural statistics, has just finished calculating the size of this year's cherry crop."

"Do you know the number?" he asks, with some interest. "Can we go public with it?"

Knowing where this is heading, I reply, "I don't know what the number is."

"Well, can we find out from Shpitzer?"

With a saddened expression, I say, "Unfortunately, after such a herculean effort to come up with the projection, Yankel simply had to take a holiday to give his nerves a rest."

"But," I add, "if you find that you have to say something about the crop, I would suggest that you say that the yield this year appears to be such and so."

He looks at me as if I'm crazy but says nothing. I know that deep in his heart he suspects that all is not kosher but he's afraid to ask. And with that he leaves.

I pour myself another cup of coffee. I consider that thank God I managed once again to save the minister from himself. A glance at my watch tells me that it's almost lunch time and that after I eat, I'll have to go for a stroll.

So, I ask you, is this not work? You think that I sit here, in the lap of luxury, dreaming all day. You don't realize that my stomach is forever churning because of what goes on around me. On my shoulders rests the minister and the entire department. Is it any wonder that I walk around looking anxious, beaten and tormented?

Do me a favour. If you should ever come across a bureaucrat, take pity on him and give him a hug. Tell him that you thank God that he is working in his job, and not you. And that for your part, you're delighted to pay your taxes, a true bargain.

A Clash of Civilizations

All my life I've been hearing about the baby boomers. The baby boomers this. The baby boomers that. Everybody knows it all started after the Second World War. Having babies became a national sport. And before you knew it we had the biggest explosion of babies in modern history. It's a fact.

It's also a fact that all these baby boomers are now alte kakers, you'll pardon the expression. Take a look at me. A pipik out to here. Bald head. Glasses. But not just any glasses. Designer glasses. Not just any shirt. A designer shirt. This came from France and this came from Italy. My nose came from the Bronx and my chin got fixed in Miami and so on and on.

And it's no surprise because this is after all the Me generation. The ones who redefined everything. What you should smoke, even if you don't inhale. To stop all wars. To do your own thing. And not just to get any job. But the perfect job. It used to be that getting a paycheck was already something to celebrate. But for a baby boomer it had to be intrinsically satisfying. What does that even mean? It means you have to be so happy doing it that you shouldn't have to get paid. I'll work for nothing. I refuse to take a cent. Just make it intrinsically satisfying!

And they changed the whole way you bring up kids.

When I was a kid, I was terrified even to ask for anything.

"Dad, can I have allowance?"

"Allowance, why do you need allowance? When I was your age, I was supporting the whole family. I worked all day and all night and went to school the rest of the time to build a future, and you want allowance?"

The baby boomers changed all that. They knew that their kids should never suffer like they did. They knew that to bring up strong, healthy kids, the first thing you do is NEVER SAY NO. It stifles them. It can turn them, God forbid, into highway robbers or axe murderers.

You've got to make them partners. Show them respect. The kid is still in diapers and you're already negotiating.

"What's your opinion, Bobby? Do you think you should stay up past nine o'clock? Midnight, you say? Alright, maybe ten-thirty. Not late enough? You want to watch the late show. But you have to get up to go to school in the morning. Oh, you have a spare in the morning. But you're only in Grade 2. What kind of a spare? OK, midnight. But only this time. Next time you'll have to talk to your mother."

God bless them. They're the best kids in the world. They're our jewels. They're what we live for. Today they depend on us. Tomorrow we'll depend on them. Oy! Of course I'm just joking.

Now we know that every generation has its problems. Inter-generational conflict. But today we're talking about the kids of the baby boomers. They're special. Brought up by the most enlightened, best educated and wealthiest generation of parents the world has ever seen. Designer parents.

So dad comes home. A hard day's work at the office where he turned the whole world on fire. He walks in the door and right away he's ambushed.

"Dad, I need the keys."

"For what?"

"Have to go out."

"Where to?"

"Dunno yet."

"Who are you going with?"

"Friends."

"Who?"

"You don't know them. Hurry up, Dad, I'm late. And I need some money."

"How much do you need?"

"Two hundred bucks. Just in case."

"Are you crazy? What are you going to do with two hundred bucks?"

"Come on, Dad. You're holding me up. Are you giving it to me or not?"

He needs the money and he's giving me ultimatums.

"OK. I'll give you a hundred but bring me change."

And poof, he's gone.

You think that mothers have it any easier?

"I'm coming home late."

"What time?"

"Late, and I'm bringing a friend."

"Who?"

"You don't know her. I just met her."

"And you're bringing her home?"

"She needs a place to crash."

"But Bobby, we've never even met her."

"Don't worry, she'll stay in my room."

"What?"

"She can sleep with me. It's no problem."

"No problem? What are you talking about?"

"I said she'll sleep with me. We won't make any noise. And in the morning she'll go home."

"She can't sleep with you. Not in our house."

"Oh, I know what you're worried about. Don't worry. We wouldn't do anything."

"I'll have to talk to your father."

"Whatever. I've gotta go."

And poof, he's gone.

So people ask me, how long does this last? What's the solution? There is no solution. Being a parent is a chronic condition.

You know I'm right because it's a fact that more and more our sons and daughters are staying home. Longer and longer. They have to find their identity. Figure out where they came from and where they're going. And you can't interfere.

"So, Bobby, any thoughts of growing up?"

"Dad, you're pressuring me. I'm only twenty-two."

Every year it's the same thing. I'm only twenty-two. I'm only thirty five. I'm only, I'm only.

And while he's figuring, you're going broke.

"Bobby, what are all these charges on my Visa?"

"I had to get some things."

"But you used my Visa. You can go to jail for that!"

"I needed the money."

"You needed the money so you stole my Visa?"

"You would have said no. What else could I do?"

It's not that they're lazy. Don't get me wrong. If they get a call from somebody important, they're off like a shot. In a split second. Running. Phoning. Organizing. Schlepping.

And every important person is called, "Yeo."

The phone rings.

"Hello... Yeo, what's up? Three in the morning? No problem. I'll be there."

For my funeral he would be late but if Yeo needs him, three in the morning is no problem.

And then, "Dad, I need a lift."

"It's late and if you go out now, you won't get up in the morning."

"Don't bug me, Dad. Just give me a lift."

"No, you'll miss school."

"Dad, you know what, just stay out of my life." Slams the door and he's off.

Just then, from out of nowhere, your wife appears. Your son's greatest advocate and defender in the whole world.

She gives you the look and asks, "What happened? What did you say to him?"

Sir

Retirement is full of surprises. This time it arrived wrapped in my brother-in-law's weekly escape from the cleaning lady. "I can't stand being there with all the fussing going on," he had lamented months earlier, "I have to get away." I had no objection to what followed. His intolerance of "the fussing" became synonymous with impromptu visits to my house, unannounced but predictable, like clockwork, every Thursday morning.

I heard the familiar thud of the car door closing in the driveway. As always, he let himself in, this time as I sat at my computer, clearing out some old emails.

The energy with which he bounded up the stairs told me that something was up. "What's new?" I asked matter-of-factly as he settled into a chair.

"Nothing," he pretended, the grin on his face giving him away. I waited for him to continue.

"Well, actually," he began, still smiling, "I've just finished scanning five thousand slides into my computer." Seeing that he'd gotten my attention, he added, "and now I can put together any photo album I want to." I may have been too harsh, but all that seemed to be missing was "so there..."

I looked at him in amazement, not sure whether I should congratulate him or pity him because he'd lost his mind.

"Five thousand slides?" I asked in as muted astonishment as I could manage.

"Yup," he replied proudly. "It took me about a year to get it done. Scanners are incredibly slow. I could only do one picture at a time and because I turned on 'dust removal', the scanning took forever." I had a vague recollection that he had mentioned something to me before about this project but the sheer magnitude of it hadn't registered. Imagining him now, sitting there hour upon hour in his dimly lit room, only his computer screen for light, killing his eyes and his back, made me wince.

"You're a patient guy," I replied. "That's a major achievement. I'm sure that I couldn't have done it. Just organizing a few shots from last summer on my computer is about all I can handle. I don't dare to think of the mountains of pictures I have in hard copy."

"Well, if you ever want my help..."

"No thanks," I replied a bit too quickly, adding, "I'm just not as patient as you."

I tucked the conversation away in the appropriate mental bin and made no more of it. That afternoon, I embarked on my mission to the butcher to buy a turkey for the holidays. As I handed over my credit card with customary good cheer and generous helpings of good wishes, I leaned forward discreetly, not wanting to reveal my age, and asked the cashier in a hushed voice if someone would be kind enough to help me carry the eighteen-pound bird to my car.

"Of course," came the eager reply, instantly betraying me to the entire line of people standing behind me. I smiled at the next couple, trying valiantly to mask my embarrassment. "I'll page Jack," the cashier continued, "he'll be happy to help you."

In minutes, a young man in his twenties arrived smiling, a white apron tied neatly around his waist, his arms swinging jauntily. He grasped the turkey in one hand and off he went.

I walked along beside him, Jack politely slowing his pace to let me keep up. I marvelled at how effortless this was for him. Grateful, without raising my eyes from the pavement, I commented, "You know, Jack, I used to be able to carry a bird just like that, no problem. Now, with my heart, it's too hard."

He glanced at me, smiling sympathetically, and replied, "I hope I even make it to your age."

My heart, such as it is, was beating just fine until that moment. "What?!" I thought, feeling my face turn red, "make it to my age?" Uninvited images flashed before my eyes. Recollections of the day, long ago, when a kindly cashier pronounced, in as sweet a voice as you could ever imagine, that single word that shortened my life, "Will that be all, SIR?"

I recalled another time, getting onto a city bus, the nice young lady who couldn't have been much younger than me getting up and asking politely, "Would you like to sit here, SIR?" I had shuddered, thinking, "Do I look that old and feeble?"

"No, I'm fine, thanks," I had replied, puffing up my chest and straightening my shoulders, as I tightened my grip on the safety bar. I had felt as if a thousand eyes were secretly looking me over, sizing me up for themselves.

And now this.

"I'm sure you'll make it way past my age," I said. "You young people will live forever."

He smiled appreciatively, not a clue about my sarcasm, as I handed him a tip.

As I drove home, my brother-in-law crept back into my mind. "Five thousand slides," I could hear him saying. I shook my head. But a thought took hold and seemed to grow that maybe, just maybe, it was time to pay our own pictures a visit, the albums my wife and I had stored away that we never touched, the boxes of photographs taken so lovingly still in their envelopes and the countless trays of slides.

Maybe, just maybe, it was time... Sir.

On Reflection

An Appeal to World Jewry

Remarks made at the closing plenary session of the Conference of the World Federation of Fighters, Partisans and Camp Inmates, Tel Aviv, 1977

The defeat of Nazi Germany in 1945 marked the end of mass murder and signalled, especially for the Jewish People, a new hope for a world free of persecution and destruction.

Today, however, we witness the birth of neo-Nazism, sympathy for the remaining Nazi criminals, distortions of justice in international bodies, tolerance of terrorism, shortsightedness in government leadership and a general readiness to forget the past.

Survivors and their children are awakening to the present realities and to the urgency of today's task. The Holocaust demonstrated the depths to which mankind can go – the burden of proof is now on those who argue that it cannot happen again.

The solemn duty belongs to us as it does to no one else – we must act with collective foresight. Our first priority must be education and education first on the Holocaust. Only if future generations have an understanding of what happened and why, can we ever hope to achieve a world free of persecution for Jews and non-Jews alike. And only with an understanding of the Holocaust can Jews today appreciate the importance of the State of Israel and freedom for Jews in the world at large.

The appeal goes out to all Jewish communities and organizations around the world, that they immediately assume responsibility for a full-scale educational offensive.

The victims died wanting above all to be remembered,
Survivors today want desperately to tell,
The world must listen,
For the sake of the future even more than the past.

A Tribute to Earth Hour

Presented at the Beth Tzedec Synagogue, in Toronto, to commemorate Earth Hour in March of 2012

It is not entirely well known that in the early 1900s, some Jewish farming colonies were established on the Canadian prairies. One of these was the Sonnenfeld Colony in the midst of which was a tiny hamlet named after its founders, Mayer and Israel Hoffer, distant relatives of mine. In its earliest years, this colony, like other frontier Jewish settlements, offered young Jewish men and women the opportunity to become masters of their own fate in Canada, in ways that they simply could not have done in the countries of their origin in Eastern Europe.

A second set of immigrants arrived in the colony immediately after the Second World War. My parents and my two older brothers, survivors of Transnistria and I, born right after the war, were among these more recent arrivals. Altogether, we were a community of some twenty Jewish families.

Although the challenges facing pioneers in the early 1900s can only be imagined, life for us, even 50 years later, was harsh. We lived in a farmhouse made of wood boards, with no furnace to battle the 40-below-zero temperatures, no electricity, no telephone and no indoor plumbing. We got our drinking water from a well at the bottom of the hill that our house stood on, a feat that involved carrying each pail uphill over snowdrifts in the bitter cold and biting wind.

But nature rewarded us with untold beauty as well. The rooster crowing at each break of dawn; the bright, blinding sun in the still of the morning; the gentle breeze that gathered the scent of budding crops and enveloped us in a cocoon of comfort and promise; the crimson sunsets; the Milky Way that glistened across a boundless sky; the majestic Northern Lights that draped us in a curtain of rainbows in the night. These were all miracles of nature.

There were other treats too for a young and fascinated mind. Watching my father milk the cow and scooping a drink right out of the milk pail; seeing him gather the cream and tirelessly stir it with a wooden spoon until it turned to butter; studying his every move as he carefully hollowed out raw potatoes, filling the cavities with oil and fashioning our own miracle of Chanukah.

And my mother braiding challahs on Friday morning, coating them lovingly with a chicken feather dipped in egg, her outstretched hands gathering the light of the Shabbos candles and blessing them in a house dimly lit by coal oil lamps but bright with affection and gratitude.

Still other things characterized life in our small Jewish community.

Occasional gatherings at our house where the favourite contest among the men was a card game called whist; where my father entertained the others who were more inclined to listen to him read stories from the Yiddish newspaper that came to us all the way from New York; where the anticipated refreshment was "vursht" sandwiches made of rye bread and salami imported all the way from Winnipeg.

Then there were the High Holidays, when my father walked the country roads for miles to our skeletal synagogue in Hoffer and somehow found the strength to lead the prayers.

The *Jewish Hour* that we listened to on the car radio every Sunday morning, our window to the Jewish world.

And Yiddish, spoken by everyone, freely, fluently, in sorrow and in joy. A language that we had not yet lost.

These, as much as the wonders of nature, were the roots that nourished and shaped us.

Earth Hour is a precious idea. It is a reminder of the importance of being mindful and deliberate so that we will treasure all that makes us who we are, in nature and in life.

Bereishit:
A Lesson in Mindfulness

D'var Torah, Beth Tzedec Men's Club, October 4, 2018

Do you remember the movie The Sunshine Boys with Walter Matthau and George Burns? In the movie, Matthau's nephew, a young executive, comes to visit his old uncle somewhere In Manhattan. As they walk along the bustling street, Matthau suggests that they have lunch. His nephew says, "I've already had lunch." To which Matthau replies, "Maybe you ate, but you didn't have lunch."

Too often we just eat, instead of having lunch. We are caught up in an achievement-oriented society in which our bodies and minds are constantly rushing through life rather than living it. Hopes, regrets, frustrations, fears, the future, the past, become one messy bundle that our minds navigate like a pin-ball machine, flitting from one target to another.

Our parsha for the week is Bereishit. We know the story, but as I thought about the parsha, I wondered what, if anything, existed before creation. I'm sure that this has been the subject of a good deal of debate, but I found it interesting that a piece I recently read concluded that "the pre-creation cosmos was filled with matter, energy, and motion." In other words, at least according to this writer, there was not nothingness. There was, in the great void, a good deal of activity. But it was chaotic, unordered and seemingly without a purpose. A helter skelter similar perhaps to the chaos in our own lives.

Making order out of chaos was the great challenge that G-d faced. How did He do it, and is there a lesson in it for us?

Let's take a look.

First, G-d remarkably chose not to create the world in one fell swoop, but to do so one day at a time, over a period of six days.

This is important because by taking six individual days, G-d gave Himself the opportunity at each stage of the process to observe and, as the Torah tells us, He "saw" that it was "good." Without the days being divided one from the other, there would have been no such pause for reflection.

But there is more to it. Simply having the opportunity to "see" was not enough. What was even more important was that G-d actually took the opportunity and "saw." And that precisely is the lesson for us. We too have the opportunity to "see" what we have done and all else around us. But do we take that opportunity as He did? G-d stopped to appreciate his work, to assure himself that each element of what He had created was "good" in itself as well as in harmony with all the other parts. If it was beneficial for Him to be mindful and in the moment, how much more beneficial would it be for us in our lives?

I'd like to offer another thought on the subject of mindfulness. A short poem I wrote goes like this:

First Flower
I saw it then,
Not at a fleeting glance,
But truly saw it, in all its splendour
And filled my lungs 'til I could breathe no more.

Too often, if we "see" at all, it is only as the poem says, "at a fleeting glance" as we try to get on with things, rushing to the next experience and the one after that. But like G-d, we have a choice. We can choose to "truly see it" and appreciate its splendour, whether it's a flower, an office tower under construction, the book we are reading, or a job well done. Life can be rich if we live in the moment, whatever that moment offers us. It can flourish if we hold it in our hands like a fragile treasure, not like just another disposable object.

So, to summarize. G-d was deliberate. He stopped to appreciate what he had done at every step of the way. The lesson for us is to do likewise. To take our time and be conscious of what we are doing and what we are experiencing. And then to go on. Because we do have to go on. Having sinned in the Garden of Eden, we do not have the luxury of simply lying in repose and reflecting. We have to toil and face the multitude of challenges that life throws at us. But here's the point. We may no longer be in the Garden of Eden, but the spirit of the Garden of Eden can still inhabit our lives if, while we toil, we truly appreciate the moment in which we live, mindful of ourselves and of the world around us.

The lesson is there in the opening lines of the Torah. We have only to be willing to learn.

A Meditation

As I pray for a year of life and blessing, may G-d grant me
the humility to know that I am only one among many,
the strength to make a difference for good,
the tenderness of spirit to care for the needy,
the wisdom to embrace differences,
the courage to confront evil,
the insight to know that what I do affects others,
the understanding to treasure the beauty and bounty of this world,
the trust to have faith in the future,
and the inspiration to give life meaning.

Elul 5772 / September 2012

CPSIA information can be obtained
at www.ICGtesting.com
Printed in the USA
BVHW082025251021
619820BV00010B/367